PRAISE FOR *WALK WITH YOUR WOLF*

'An important message about the power of reconnecting with the primal self to achieve balance in the modern world. A fascinating read.'

Megan Hine, author, wilderness guide and survival consultant

'Jonathan Hoban challenges us to use nature as a setting for reconsidering our lives and our stresses. He asks us to 'walk alongside our difficulties' giving ourselves the physical and mental space to look at ourselves anew and to decide what we really need. For that commute to work, or indeed for that break on the park bench, I commend his book.'

Sir Ciarán Devane, CEO of the British Council

'Combining therapy with nature and activity isn't new. In the late 1900s, Sigmund Freud walked with certain of his patients around the Ringstrasse, Vienna's grand, tree-lined boulevard. But what if you have no therapist or kindred spirit to accompany you? Jonathan Hoban's original, inspiring and powerful book fills the gap. Deftly blending science, his own narrative and his experience as a therapist, he is at our side as we find a way of engaging with and being healed by nature. Like the wolf in the book's title, we can reconnect with our own elemental lupine instincts which are so often repressed in our stressful and artificial world – both a wolf's wildness as well as its sociability and need to be part of a pack. Follow in Hoban's easy to apply footsteps and you will never walk alone again.'

Rachel Kelly, bestselling author of *Walking on Sunshine* and *The Happy Kitchen*

ABOUT THE AUTHOR

Photograph © Timi Eross

Jonathan Hoban is a leading London-based psychotherapist who has pioneered a unique therapeutic approach known as Walking Therapy. This style of therapy, combining a walk in nature – in the countryside or in green city spaces – with counselling, has led to astonishing improvements in his clients, who range from stressed-out corporate executives to celebrities to members of the general public. He runs residential 'Burn Out' retreats in rural Isle of Wight where people can clear their body and mind.

His work has been featured in print, digital and broadcast media, including the BBC, The *Daily Telegraph*, *You* Magazine and *Women's Health*. He is a professionally registered member of the British Association for Counselling and Psychotherapy (BACP).

Find out more at www.jonathanhoban.com.

WALK WITH YOUR WOLF

UNLOCK YOUR INTUITION, CONFIDENCE & POWER

JONATHAN HOBAN

yellow
kite

First published in Great Britain in 2019 by Yellow Kite
An imprint of Hodder & Stoughton
An Hachette UK company

1

A CIP catalogue record for this title is available from the British Library

Trade Paperback ISBN 978 1 473 69321 0
eBook ISBN 978 1 473 69323 4

Typeset in Minion Pro by Palimpsest Book Production Ltd, Falkirk, Stirlingshire

Printed and bound in Great Britain by Clays Ltd, Elcograf S.p.A.

Hodder & Stoughton policy is to use papers that are natural, renewable and recyclable products and made from wood grown in sustainable forests. The logging and manufacturing processes are expected to conform to the environmental regulations of the country of origin.

Yellow Kite
Hodder & Stoughton Ltd
Carmelite House
50 Victoria Embankment
London EC4Y 0DZ

www.yellowkitebooks.co.uk

www.hodder.co.uk

In loving memory of Mavis, Richard and John Hoban

CONTENTS

INTRODUCTION

We were almost three-quarters of the way through our second counselling session and Victoria still hadn't looked me in the eye. Almost every sign of stress and anxiety was visible in the tight, protective way she sat in the chair, and in the few words she spoke. Clearly, she didn't want to be here; equally clearly, she needed help.

The room was grey and cheerless, as counselling rooms typically are. I'd noticed that many of my clients felt the same way as Victoria; uncomfortable in these surroundings and reluctant to engage. I could see that she was feeling under immense pressure, and that this was causing her even more anxiety and stress.

I thought back to where I felt most comfortable during difficult periods in my own life. And it wasn't in a closed environment like this, but outdoors among trees and in parks. Nature became what I thought of as a 'universal parent' in the way it guided, carried and nurtured me with its presence through some of the most troubled moments of my life. Walking in nature gave me clarity, and the space to listen to myself. It didn't judge or distract, and it connected me to my environment and my feelings. Because of the honesty and perspective it provided, I knew that if I sought it out, it would always be there for me unconditionally and I would never be alone again.

In short, it saved my life.

I looked at Victoria. She was miserable, scared and defensive, her body twisted into the chair opposite me.

'You're finding this really hard, aren't you?' I said.

Victoria nodded. 'I've done all this stuff before, when I was younger, and it didn't work then. I hate it.'

'You feel that you just can't open up in here.'

She nodded again. I saw she was on the verge of tears.

'OK. I'll tell you what . . . next week, let's not meet here. Let's go out for a walk instead. Do you know Wimbledon Park?'

Victoria looked up and, for the first time, seemed to visibly relax.

'Yes,' she said. 'That'd be great. Let's do it.'

So we did. And that was the start of Victoria's journey to recovery.

As a society, we're suffering from a full-blown epidemic of stress, anxiety and depression. You know this, because you're one of the people affected, or because you know someone who is. You feel you've neither the space nor the time to relax, unwind and simply 'be'. Your phone bleeps constantly. There seems no end to the emails you must answer. Your work environment is frenetic. Everyone is wired on caffeine. There is not a moment to spare; not a minute where your 'performance' isn't being appraised and monitored. The pressure is on, constantly and relentlessly.

We all feel this, yet we collaborate in keeping it at boiling point. We're seeing burnout on an unprecedented scale, and yet we are all complicit in it. How many of us dare say no, we *won't* work beyond our hours, or yes, we *are* having a lunch break and no, we're *not* giving in to any more unreasonable demands from increasingly stressed-out managers?

Rather, we attempt desperately to carve out some 'me-time'

amid this maelstrom of stress. We cram in a whistle-stop city break here, a pointless work trip there; we sit glumly on a packed beach, wishing those noisy kids playing near by would clear off, or we go on a yoga retreat and find we can't stop crying. Our feelings are rarely far from the surface and yet we push them down with all the force of someone cramming rubbish into an overflowing dustbin or hide them away like clutter in the attic that we don't want to see, yet somehow can't bear to be parted from. We cannot – and do not want to – engage with them, because to do so feels unnerving, unfamiliar and maybe even dangerous. So we continue to perform at work while self-medicating with drink, drugs, sex, fast food, intensive gym workouts, hours of therapy and whatever else it might take to keep ourselves pacified. And this vicious circle keeps repeating itself.

The solution . . .

. . . is simple. It involves no joining fees, no memberships, no appointments. It does, however, require time, patience, an ability to switch off (literally) and a desire to reconnect with that which is all around you.

The solution is to go for a walk. Not a stroll down the pub or a pop to the shops, but a good stride out that gets body and mind moving, allowing you to de-stress, see what's important and find perspective in all the difficulties and challenges life presents.

When you walk, you find the space to process your feelings and begin to understand that nature is your greatest healer. By being outside in nature, whatever the weather, you will re-establish the vital and fundamental connection to the earth that we were all born with but have somehow lost. You will also learn how to relax and how to listen to what your intuition is telling you without all the 'noise' that usually blocks it out.

The beauty of what I term 'Walking Therapy' is in its simplicity. All you need to do is make time to put one foot in front of the other, in a space which calms the mind, invigorates the senses and helps you to walk alongside your difficulties, seeing them for what they are.

And it's important to note that 'nature' is not confined to wild, remote and inaccessible places. It is everywhere, even in the most urban areas, if you care to look. The great cities of the world, including London, contain many amazing parks and other open spaces in which it is perfectly possible to feel close to the earth and connected to the environment. It is on your doorstep, and it invites you in with open arms. The trick is in responding to its call. If you do, wonderful things will happen.

How does this book work?

Although Walking Therapy has simplicity at its heart, it is not a quick fix. It is about consistency, determination, mindfulness, resilience and awareness. To engage with the process, you need to be on your toes – physically and mentally. You will need to walk regularly and accept that healing doesn't happen over-night. You already know you need help to deal with certain feelings and situations in your life, but you must be prepared to put the work in and be courageous in your approach. If you understand and accept this, the benefits of Walking Therapy include:

- stress reduction
- a more positive mood
- clarity of thinking
- reduced anxiety

- a deeper connection with the environment
- improved physical health
- less reliance on harmful substances or habits to 'get you through'
- a better relationship with yourself and with those close to you.

All that said, this is not a prescriptive book. Everyone is different, and people will go at their own pace. *Walk With Your Wolf* offers practical, up-to-the-minute advice and exercises in how to walk, think and feel as a means of confronting difficult emotions. We will start with first steps and, as your progress builds, you will begin to understand how your mind and body are responding positively to being out in nature and connecting with the elements. I will walk alongside you as a friend and guide, showing you the path to self-discovery and healing. And on the way, I will share my own story of addiction and recovery, the latter being such a positive experience that I decided to become a counsellor, hoping I could do for others what my counsellors did for me. I'll shed light, where appropriate, on my own journey and I will introduce some of my clients, whose stories will inspire you to follow in their footsteps. We will walk in response to stress, anxiety, depression, grief, addiction and life transitions, among other challenges that we all face.

This book is aimed at everyone because we are all subject to life's pressures. You are no longer alone – we will take this journey together as we repair your relationship with the world, with other people and, most importantly, with yourself.

Note: as you progress, you might choose to walk with a friend, but the first read of this book is a therapeutic journey that needs to be done solo.

Why the wolf?

We're all animals, with the potential for connecting to our instinctive, wilder side. To my mind, the wolf is an excellent metaphor for the duality of the human condition. On one hand, it represents our wildness, danger and a fear of our deepest, darkest feelings – our primal energies that react without thought and whatever is necessary for our survival. On the other, the wolf is also a highly social animal, loyal to its pack, communicative, instinctual and free. The wolf is very much my 'shadow animal'; its character traits personify certain aspects and different dimensions of my subconscious mind, self and spirit – something I'll expand on later. Similarly, its environment is vital to its well-being and survival.

Personally, I identify with the wolf's sensitivity, loyalty, intelligence and sociability around its pack. A wolf needs space to roam, just as we humans need space to 'be'. If wolves do not have enough space, their roaming and hunting instinct is broken, which can cause them huge amounts of stress. In captivity, they can no longer behave in a way that is intuitive to them, instead becoming hypervigilant – far more than they would ever be in the wild. Their fur loses its sheen and their eyes become dull. The edge is taken off their sensitivity and although they eventually accept their new situation, they are not the same creatures they were before confinement.

Recognise any parallels here? Is this similar to how you're feeling? It is your space which the twenty-first century seems determined to encroach upon. As humans, we need to reclaim the wildness within each of us. As they say, 'Throw me to the wolves and I'll return leading the pack'.

What happens when we are confined?

When we spend most of our time either at work or thinking about it even when we're not physically in the workplace, our levels of cortisol – the stress hormone – are raised. Stress levels that are permanently high lead to poor decision-making, a lack of perspective, impatience and anxiety, depression, addiction (to your own adrenalin, which is also elevated in times of stress, as well as external elements, such as drink or drugs), mental illness . . . the list goes on. We find ourselves in constant 'fight, flight or freeze' mode, as our bodies desperately scramble to catch up with the unrelenting stress we're putting ourselves through. We lose all sense of personal boundaries and we completely forget that we, as human animals, need nurturing.

In short, we've abandoned ourselves. And in my experience, the worst trauma occurs not when we're abandoned by others, but when we abandon ourselves.

How do you think you might have abandoned yourself? Perhaps by no longer doing a hobby you used to enjoy, or by not spending time with people who aren't associated with your work? Maybe you've abandoned yourself to overeating, by drinking alcohol to excess or by getting involved in toxic relationships? Or simply by working too hard for too long. Take a moment now to consider the areas of your life in which personal abandonment could be happening.

By highlighting these areas, hopefully you'll see where your life has become unmanageable. It's important to note that a lack of manageability, plus the loss of personal boundaries and the inability to say 'No' or 'Stop' can create indecisiveness, insecurity and stress in day-to-day life. And if you're stressed for prolonged periods of time, you lose personal clarity and end up feeling trapped and powerless. Rediscovering personal clarity and honesty, plus learning how to manage the factors that cause stress, are the key drivers behind this book.

It is time to stop abandoning yourself and turn your focus on nurturing those parts you've neglected. And, in some ways, to learn how to be selfish. This is a word that is sometimes used to shame those who will not slavishly serve the needs of others. But are you selfish because you'd rather go to the cinema alone than head to the pub with your friends or work colleagues? Are you selfish because you take an hour outdoors for lunch while everyone else is eating at their desks? No, of course you're not – so don't let anyone shame you into thinking that way. Instead, think of it as 'self-care'. Other people's opinions of you don't matter; it's what you believe and feel intuitively that counts. Too easily can you abandon how you truly feel to the control of others.

Walking your way to happiness

We've seen what the dangers of frequently raised cortisol and adrenalin levels are. But there is an antidote: oxytocin. Sometimes known as the 'love drug', because it is associated with mother–baby bonding, touch, intimacy, smiling, laughing and many other ways of feeling good (including walking), oxytocin is released when we walk, along with endorphins, and almost immediately we feel the benefits as the hormones rush around the body. In fact, a 2015 study carried out at the Stanford Woods Institute for the Environment in California found that people who walked for ninety minutes in a natural area showed decreased activity in a region of the brain related to a key factor in depression.[1] So moving in nature makes us feel good and acts as a de-stressor, allowing us the time and space to process thoughts and feelings, as well as enabling us to think clearly.

Walking is very often a natural, instinctive solution to a pressing problem. How many of us have said, 'That's it, I'm going for a walk!' when we're faced with conflict or a difficult decision to make? And how many of us come back with a solution, or at least something approaching clarity? Most, I'd suspect.

Can walking really solve all your problems?

As I've said, we're not talking about a quick fix. You might walk to the supermarket and back, but that isn't really going to solve anything. You have to move – really move. I'm not suggesting a hike to the top of the nearest mountain (well, not yet), but if you really want to get your brain activity flowing, you do need to get out there, in all weathers, and immerse yourself in the experience of walking in nature.

When you decide to go for a walk, you're also making adequate time in your busy life to process your thoughts and feelings. Becoming consciously aware of how you're feeling before, during and after each walk can help you get used to 'naming' how you feel. This naming of feelings (for example, 'I feel happy', 'I feel anxious', 'I feel melancholy', 'I feel sad') helps your brain and body to manage your thoughts and emotions more effectively.

Identifying and naming emotions can also help to externalise feelings that you often internalise without knowing or choose not to share out of fear of feeling vulnerable and exposed. Finding a voice to name and make explicit emotions you experience, both to yourself and others, expands your emotional vocabulary and awareness, improves confidence and self-esteem, alleviates emotional and physical stress and provides you with a much-needed feeling of release and relief. There is no shame in naming your feelings, but it may take some getting used to if it's not something you already do.

When you're moving physically, you start to think with much more clarity; and when you're walking through nature, you are re-forging a spiritual and emotional connection to nature that you've allowed yourself to lose.

When I was growing up, I was always 'the sensitive one'. That was my label. People think I'm very confident, but I can be painfully shy and sensitive. As soon as Jonathan and I started walking, I very quickly noticed myself changing. By getting outside and going for a walk before work, the rest of my day would be a good one. I was calming down and beginning to really understand myself. I stopped drinking and going out so much, and everything was getting better. I learned how to talk to myself. It gave me something to concentrate on. All I knew before was that I had no idea how my mind worked, except that it let me down all the time.'

Victoria

My aim is that by the end of this book you will have returned to the person you were born to be. It's an ambitious aim, for sure, but my mission is to get you feeling *alive* again. Walking will stimulate your senses and invigorate you, body and soul. By returning to the person you were meant to be – instead of feeling stressed, anxious, depressed or burnt out – you will find peace, knowing that you have the ability to be truly honest with yourself and the personal clarity you've been longing for. So can walking really solve your problems? Yes, it can, because when this happens, you will be in a much better position to make the changes you need for a healthier, happier life.

CHAPTER 1: A BEAST CALLED STRESS

When all is lost, something wild will find you.
A Monster Calls, 2016, adapted from the book by Patrick Ness

So where do we go from here? Outdoors, obviously! But first, we'll look at what's going on for you right now, plus some initial steps towards learning how to walk consciously, mindfully and with your personal healing at the forefront of the exercise.

And before we do all that, I'm going to do something that very few therapists ever do – that is to tell you something about myself and my struggles in life. 'This is your time and space,' they usually say, 'and you can bring to it whatever you need to explore and discuss.' Which is fine, of course, and how it should be – except that there are two people in a therapeutic space.

Historically, the onus has always been on the client to take all the risks by disclosing intimate details about their life experiences, only to receive minimal responses and emotional input from their therapist. This is a pity, however, because as therapists, we learn as much from our clients as they do from us; it's a two-way exchange of life experiences which collectively enrich the therapeutic relationship, helping both parties to expand their knowledge base.

I've found that when I've talked to clients about my own past, they've felt a sense of relief from knowing that someone else has been through something similar they can relate to. Identifying with another's experience is extremely powerful and can really help a person not to feel isolated and alone during their time of adversity. As a therapist, I think it's useful to disclose my story and to share extracts from my own life experience, but only if relevant to the topic of discussion and the ongoing growth of the therapeutic relationship. Boundaries between client and therapist must still exist, but at the same time, a relationship is a relationship. So given that I'm sharing this journey with you, here's a bit of background about the earlier years of my life.

My story

I grew up in south-west London, the youngest of four, in a highly academic family. My father was fifty when I was born. He was what you'd call a 'true gentlemen'; he served in the Royal Navy in World War Two and afterwards went into publishing and broadcast journalism at the BBC. He was a religious man and passionate about sacred music, which led to him becoming Director of Music at the Brompton Oratory in west London. My mother was Irish, a professional opera singer who always surrounded us with music and was a wonderful, loving parent to us all. As a child, I remember her telling me stories of mystical and mythical worlds, with a heavy emphasis on fantasy and the supernatural. It's no wonder I grew up a dreamer, outlandish in my behaviour and with a crazy imagination. But I thank her for teaching me how to be explorative, and to always harbour big dreams.

My siblings were academic and went to top schools. I was different. I was slightly dyslexic, extremely sensitive and a free spirit, and didn't fit into the competitive world of educa-tion. I loved life, but also feared it greatly. I didn't know how to act or be. I suffered from shyness, anxiety, low self-esteem and a lack of confidence, none of which was helped by persistent bullying at school that left me constantly stressed. I attended several schools but made very little progress at any of them. Fear engulfed me daily, and I couldn't seem to escape it wherever I went.

When I was twelve, my mother was diagnosed with colon cancer and after a five-year struggle she died. During her fight against the illness, I gradually stopped caring about anything school-related and started drinking to numb the pain. I walked out of school shortly after my mother died, as life was too short to be miserable in a place where I clearly didn't belong. After many failed attempts at modelling and acting, I decided to join a band and started writing songs, having inherited both my parents' musical abilities. I'd finally found a lifestyle which gave me a true sense of belonging; and my love of alcohol and other recreational drugs slotted nicely into the identity I had created for myself as a rock musician.

Five years later, the day after the anniversary of my mother's death, my brother Richard was found dead in his house at the age of thirty-two from a methadone overdose. Growing up, we'd always had a deep understanding of each other and losing him, together with the loss of my mother, had a huge effect upon my life. Witnessing my father's heartbreak at losing his wife to cancer, followed by the sudden death of his firstborn son, is also something I'll never forget. Needless to say, this added to my trauma.

To put it bluntly, I just didn't care any more. I fell deeper into recreational drug-taking; at one point, before I got clean, I was taking seven grams of cocaine and drinking around forty units of alcohol a day. I put myself in many dark, dangerous situations and, in all honesty, I'm lucky to be alive.

My addiction was no longer a joke, and flippant comments I had previously made to lighten the situation, such as, 'I never had a blackout on the nights I can remember,' had fallen by the wayside. I was truly lost.

Two people saved me. The first was my then manager, Ronan O'Rahilly, founder of Radio Caroline, who had an unwavering belief in me. He told me many times I was like the son he never had, while for me, he was very much the surrogate father figure and role model I needed at the time. He consistently reminded me that I wasn't stupid (I'd always assumed I was because I wasn't academic) and he allowed me to express my feelings of anger without judgement. As Ronan was a born rebel himself, he embraced my anarchy rather than fearing it and because of this I was always free to voice my opinions and felt truly valued.

The second person was a young boy whose name I do not know. At twenty-three, I was scruffy, bearded and addicted to drink and drugs. One day, I was sitting on the street, coming down off a two-day cocaine bender, when a woman and her son passed by. The little boy stopped, looked at me and said, 'Mummy, is he OK?' And I'll never forget that moment. A light was suddenly switched on inside me. Because this child saw right through my outward appearance and, with pure empathy, he reignited a hopeful and loving part of me that I'd disconnected from. It was weird. By simply acknowledging me that day, and without any judgement in his eyes, he made me feel like I was a worthy human being, not a worthless piece of dirt. That singular moment and human loving exchange gave me strength and clarity.

Immediately, I realised I'd had enough of my way of life, and knew I needed to change. It was do or die. I went into rehab, underwent counselling and finally got clean.

Overall, I had a good childhood with loving parents, but one of the core issues that came out of my personal therapy was the trauma of never feeling I was truly seen or heard. And because of this I felt alone, misunderstood and angry. I also learned that I had major issues with authority figures and an acute reluctance to take personal responsibility for anything in my life. I had trust issues and problems forming close relationships, as I felt everyone would either eventually leave me or let me down. In short, I was still incredibly anxious, stressed out, with no real idea of who I was or where I was going. So I did what I'm now asking you to do – I instinctively put one foot in front of the other and started walking regularly, usually on Wimbledon Common and in Richmond Park.

Walking every day and immersing myself in nature gave me the strength to rebuild my life. Stepping among the trees, I felt a true sense of belonging and connection to an energy that was looking after and supporting me. As I walked, I became aware that I was part of something bigger, wilder and more powerful than I was; something that would protect, nurture and provide me with a deep perspective. It was then that I realised that nature was my universal parent. And ever since, I have spent time building that relationship.

As a result of my mother's and brother's deaths, love was taken away from me at a young age, but I rediscovered it in the trees, fields and parks I walked in. Nature didn't judge or ask anything of me; it simply allowed me to wrap myself in it. I had been crushed by everything that had happened to me, and how I'd reacted to it, but nature took me by the hand and guided me through many different types of emotional weathers to a place where I felt peaceful and in control of my life once again. Walking provided me with a neutral space in which to discover who I was becoming, dispelling the 'noise' in my psyche. That allowed me to connect with and observe my thoughts and feelings with true clarity, as wild and scary as they were at times.

We all belong to nature, and if we open our arms to it, it will do the same for us.

Stress, society and you

For many of us, the world we live in now bears little resemblance to that of the past – even a past as recent as a decade ago. The internet and social media have changed our working environment and personal lives irrevocably. We now strive to exist in a place where the pressure to perform is strong, and it's not just about doing our jobs, but being 'seen' to be doing them. We're always 'on', always poised to respond. There's no let-up at times for breaks, a cup of tea or even a moment to catch our breath.

As the climate of technology changes within our society, we are subconsciously forced to keep pace with current trends. However much we check, check, check, we never seem able to keep up with the demands of work or the pressure social media places upon us. As a result, our self-esteem suffers greatly as we compare ourselves to those who seem to be more popular or more successful or whoever we *presume* is 'doing better' than we are, even though this is often not the case.

We can, of course, turn everything off and walk away. But for how long? Technology and work stress are insidious – there is always something that requires answering, updating or commenting on. And there is the famed 'FOMO' – Fear Of Missing Out. We condemn teenagers for their phone addiction, but really, are we as adults any better or wiser?

The demands that a faster, hypertech society force upon us have led to an overdose of stress. According to the Mental Health

Foundation, stress is damaging the health of millions of people around the UK; it is, they say, 'one of the great public health challenges of our time but it is not being taken as seriously as physical health concerns'.[2]

Stress is a primal response to anything we see as a 'threat', putting us into fight, flight or freeze mode. Thousands of years ago, this threat might have shown itself in the form of wild animals or people from other tribes who were hunting or trying to kill us. The source of 'threat' has changed over time, of course, but our response remains largely the same – we switch to a high-alert mode as our bodies release adrenalin, norepinephrine and cortisol to prepare us for the decision we must make: whether to stand our ground (fight), run away (flight) or do nothing (freeze).

In the short term, this response is helpful, as it focuses our decision-making. But when we're constantly faced with 'threats' (a heavy workload, never-ending demands at home, a long to-do list and all-seeing social media) and our adrenalin and cortisol levels are always raised, we're very prone to the damaging effects of stress. Higher levels of stress – both short- and longer-term – force the brain into a state of tunnel vision and we lose sight of what is on the periphery of our lives. This inevitably creates consequences and issues within our familial and social lives, as we slowly lose a sense of what's real, important and meaningful. We also lose our sense of personal clarity and start making poor decisions. And there are other symptoms too:

- Fear or anxiety
- Worry
- Racing thoughts
- Feeling overwhelmed by our responsibilities
- Feeling trapped by salary
- Irritability

- Depression
- Feeling constantly tired and depleted
- Difficulty sleeping or having stress dreams
- Overeating/undereating
- Drinking too much.

Stress is the driver for a lot of problems therapists regularly encounter with clients, leading to what we'd describe as 'burnout' – the point where the body is screaming 'enough!' According to a 2018 survey by the UK-based Mental Health Foundation think tank, three-quarters of adults have felt overwhelmed or unable to cope because of stress, and 12.5 million working days a year are lost as a result.[3,4] Multiply that by all the world's developed economies and we have a very, very big problem on our hands. In fact, the World Health Organization has described it as 'an epidemic'.

Let's hear from some of my clients now. First, from Beverley, who works in the National Health Service in a job she loves – even if the pressures are relentless.

> *Relationship-wise and family-wise, everything seemed to be breaking down because I was working thirteen hours a day and coming home extremely stressed. I've never considered myself an anxious person, but I was experiencing high levels of anxiety and started to have panic attacks on the way to work. I could feel the rising panic in my throat as I neared my workplace and I couldn't get through any day without being in tears at least once – which wasn't like me at all. And if I wasn't at work I was just at home, crying. It was awful.*
> **Beverley**

When I first met her, Beverley was typical of someone who had lost the concept of looking after themselves through prioritising her well-being and mental health. Her stress levels were so raised that her face was constantly flushed, giving me the impression that she was an alcoholic. She wasn't a drinker – it was just stress showing itself in her complexion. During that painful period, I can honestly say that she looked ten years older than she does now.

> *I was told by my GP to take three months off work, but I couldn't do it. It's a pride thing. I'm Zimbabwean and work is very important to us. If I wasn't there, who would look after the patients? Who would care for them, and my team? I felt guilty, and I couldn't think clearly about what was right for me. In hindsight, I was stupid.*
> **Beverley**

Katrina, another client, told me about her background and how pressure around her career prospects led to her abandoning herself to work:

> *I was single, in a very stressful job and had issues over lots of things, including confidence and being overweight. Generally, I just thought I didn't have much to feel good about in life. I was brought up to believe you had to have a job which made a lot of money, so I got caught up in that and forgot to have a life too. My siblings had gone through the state-school system and not done very well, so my dad paid for me to go*

*to an all-girls private school. It wasn't the best
environment for me; I felt burdened with guilt
over having to succeed, and it was a very
bullying, shaming place to be.*
Katrina

Katrina is a highly intelligent, yet very sensitive woman (which commonly go together) who had completely neglected herself, working twelve hours a day with no breaks, and over weekends. She felt trapped by the lifestyle facilitated by her salary, had lost a sense of her personal boundaries and was unable to break out of the vicious cycle in which she found herself. She was impatient to 'fix' the problem and had unrealistic expectations of how quickly this could be achieved.

Victoria, whom we met in the Introduction, had been (wrongly) diagnosed with clinical depression when she was fifteen by a general practitioner and, more than a decade later, was suffering from the consequences of that label. She was working in a high-pressure industry and had difficulties with a manager who bullied her. Victoria's way of dealing with everything was via recreational drinking, drug-taking and partying hard.

*I would hit a low where I couldn't talk to anyone.
I felt like I was heartbroken without knowing
why. My boss would upset and offend me, and
I'd just break down in tears. People think I'm
very confident, but I can be painfully shy and
sensitive. I masked it by going out all the time.
I would happily go out every night, and I'd say
'Yes' to anything. I never thought much of it –
drinking gave me the confidence I didn't have.*
Victoria

Beverley, Katrina and Victoria were all responding to high levels of stress in different ways. What ties their stories together is the fact that their ways of coping were unhealthy, unhelpful and short-term fixes. None of them had any idea of self-care and they were all very reluctant to open up within a therapy room during face-to-face counselling. All three felt extremely uncomfortable with that style of healing, yet they all recognised they had to 'do something' to alleviate their unhappiness.

First steps to base camp

Recognising that you're experiencing stress isn't difficult, and by buying this book you've already taken a first step towards understanding that it's become a problem for you, or someone you know. Dealing with it, however, involves certain actions and life changes. It requires being courageous in your vulnerability.

Sometimes it can simply be the gift of desperation that motivates you to act on your feelings. If it's work-related you could, in theory, simply get up from your desk now, walk out of the door and never return. It's a solution, right? But it's a drastic one. You still have responsibilities – there may be bills to pay, people to look after – and while these should not hinder your progress towards reconnecting with your true self, there are certain realities to consider before you take action.

The best way of tackling anything that requires challenge or change is to take small steps towards it. A common mistake among those seeking a better way of living is to make hasty, reckless decisions, only to fall on the first slippery slope. But you're not going to get to the top of the mountain straight away. At the moment, you're only approaching base camp. What you need in your life is 'manageability' – the ability to make the choices and decisions that allow you to be in control of your life. It's a lack of manageability which creates stress, arising from the inability to set boundaries, create realistic goals, to see situations clearly and to evaluate them for what they're really worth. The wolf doesn't charge at its prey blindly; it waits and considers the best moment to make its move. You are already stressed enough, and not always capable of making big decisions. Once you have established a routine of achieving small goals, you can then begin to think about and plan your first foray into therapeutic walking.

The three aspects of self you need to consider in this process are:

- psychological
- physiological
- spiritual.

These three must be upheld in order to maintain good mental health. And they all need to work in conjunction with each other, collectively, like a team, to achieve a true sense of balance and well-being. Let's look at them a little more closely in terms of the benefits that Walking Therapy delivers.

The psychological factor

When you walk for therapeutic purposes, your brain works in conjunction with your physical movements. 'Thinking on your feet' is a common expression, and a true one. When you sit for long periods, your cognitive process (pre-frontal cortex) is far slower than when you're up, outside and moving. When you sit down, the animal brain presumes you are either eating, sleeping or grooming, whereas when you're walking, it becomes far more active and productive as it believes, 'I'm hunting and thinking, I'm full of energy and life and I'm vigilant'. In addition to this, Walking Therapy promotes the release of the feel-good hormones dopamine, serotonin, endorphins and oxytocin, as well as others such as adrenalin inside the body, creating a natural high and leaving you feeling invigorated, happy and full of life.

Emotion and physical expression are essential for communication and social interaction. Your posture, gestures and the way you move – both consciously and subconsciously – inform you and others about how you are feeling. Walking helps you to relax your mind and process your feelings more effectively and it encourages you to be openly expressive in your body language. This has been one of the most noticeable differences I have seen in my Walking Therapy clients since making the transition from indoor, face-to-face sessions.

Taking a walk outside, within a natural setting, is especially beneficial because sounds, scents and scenery help us to recall memories, thoughts and feelings in the present moment.

The physiological factor

Walking is extremely good for your body. It lowers blood pressure and helps to channel out unwanted or negative feelings, reducing physical and emotional stress. Walking also helps to reduce cholesterol levels, boost metabolism and promote weight loss which, in turn, improves circulation throughout your body, carrying more oxygen and nutrients to your organs, which contributes to clearer thinking.

The physical act of walking is a necessary reminder that you need to maintain and prioritise self-care above anything else.

The spiritual factor

Some people are put off by the term 'spirituality'. Beverley was one of those who found it uncomfortable, so instead I used the words 'connection' or 'connectedness'. Whichever term you prefer, please don't be put off by the idea that Walking Therapy has a spiritual dimension. Yes, we are all made of material stuff, but to my mind, there is no denying that a human 'spirit' exists and that, by and large, we all have a primal need to connect – to each other and to nature. I make no apologies for believing this, because it is when we feel disconnected from life around us that we become destabilised and start to experience emotional difficulties. I feel that our spiritual/connected side dies when we're limited by the tunnel vision of stress, when all we focus on are the things that make us stressed, not those which could feasibly heal us.

Being in nature provides an anchoring, a grounding – an essential connection. If you're able to see and feel this, even fleetingly, while you're out walking you will understand how fundamental spirituality/connectedness is to your recovery, happiness, mental health and well-being.

Let's hear from a former client, Jerry, who really embraced the spiritual/connected side of Walking Therapy:

> So often I see the environment I'm in as a reflection of my mental state. Being in a room, being in an office, being at home with all the various pressures, particularly in a city which can be confining for most people, the immediate environment outside my body can exacerbate the state of mind that feels rather caged or hemmed in. As soon as I get outside and the

feeling lifts to the heavens, it immediately
changes my mental point of view. I feel released;
there's a feeling of possibility that comes
directly from my perception of all the space I
see, sense and feel around me.
Jerry

Take back time

By now, I've hopefully made you aware of the benefits of getting outdoors and going for a walk. But there's a problem, right? And it's one of priorities and responsibilities. You just don't have the time for all this walking stuff. You have work to do, deadlines to meet, managers to please. The kids can't get themselves to their various out-of-school activities on their own and the house-work won't do itself . . .

I understand. Time is precious, particularly if your job makes significant inroads into it. Yet by procrastinating or finding excuses not to get outdoors you're simply compounding your lack of self-care. If you're going to take walking seriously and, by extension, the task of repairing and reconnecting to your true/authentic self (that part of you that is a real reflection of your thoughts, values and beliefs), harnessing the reparative power that nature can provide you with – you really have to prioritise the necessary 'me-time' to go out and do it. You have to make the commitment to yourself, and stick to it.

I'm not asking you to climb Everest, or walk from one end of the country to the other. I just need you to say, 'This is my time now. And I'm going to manage it, and make it happen for me.' By doing so, you are already taking control and setting the boundaries that are otherwise missing from your life. Timetable your walk into your week and make it non-negotiable.

EXERCISE: TAKING TWENTY MINUTES

So to begin, let's do two simple things.

The first is to make a cup of tea or coffee and drink it without doing anything else. Or go out of the office for lunch. Or call someone you know and have a chat with them, just for the sake of it. Just do something for twenty minutes – anything that doesn't involve work, the use of technology, domestic duties or any other thing you usually feel the need to prioritise before yourself. Go outside, walk around the block, look at the sky, get some fresh air or chat to a colleague outside – and not about work. *It is imperative that you do this exercise just for you, and you alone.*

Then, secondly, when you've done this, write down what you did and how you felt in a journal or in the space provided below. Write about what it was like to put a necessary personal boundary in place for yourself, even for a short period, and ring-fence some time for you.

During my 20-minute break I ....
....
....

Afterwards, I felt ....
....
....
....

I'm scared of hitting the low points I know I can go to, but now there are a few things I do which have helped me, like having a cup of tea, calling my sister or seeing my nieces. Sometimes I have SAD (seasonal affective disorder) in the winter and will have a sunbed as a mood enhancer. Sometimes I'll just go for a run. It's hard to cry when you're running! Doing these simple, small things lifts me enough to never hit that rock bottom.

Victoria

I want you to take these brief twenty minutes for yourself a couple of times a day, *every* day. This will help you to get into the habit of self-care, while recognising that taking time out to do something small is not selfish and is actually very beneficial in the long term. You could also look at this exercise from the other end of the telescope and see what you might *not* do in order to make more time. Could that food-shopping trip or huge pile of washing be put off for another day to make way for something more life-enhancing? Could you switch off your phone and forget about social media for a while?

The other thing I'd like you to do, to ensure that you are fully invested in Walking Therapy and the exercises in this book, is to buy a pair of walking shoes or boots. The sheer act of going into a shop and getting kitted out with something suitable – both comfortable and weather-resistant – means you're physically and mentally setting yourself up for your journey. You're telling your brain that you're going to do this, and no amount of rain, mud, ice or snow will stop you. As keen walkers will say, 'There's no such thing as bad weather, just bad preparation'. Good preparation is one of the cornerstones of Walking Therapy's success, so be sure to factor in the time and equipment needed to be organised for the journey ahead.

Your commitment to these preparatory steps will help you to become more disciplined in your thinking, which will set you on the road to changing other aspects of yourself and your behaviour throughout the course of this book.

CHAPTER 2: FIRST STEPS TOWARDS YOUR TRUE SELF

If you live among wolves, you have to act like a wolf.
Nikita Khrushchev, leader of the Soviet Union, 1953–64

The wolf is a very observant creature. Like most wild animals, its sheer survival depends on its ability to watch what's going on and make decisions based on its situation, using its intuition.

In today's world, all too often we are being observed rather than observing, particularly at work. No matter how senior our position, we feel we are constantly on trial – perhaps ever more so as we climb the corporate ladder. We are rated on our 'performance', as though we are circus animals. And those who rate us face similar assessments from those above them. And so it goes on. We may then also start questioning and feeling insecure about aspects of our personal life: am I a good enough parent? Am I a good husband or wife? Who am I? All these doubts, fears and insecurities can create 'noise' in our minds and stress in our bodies, as we saw in the previous chapter. But if, for a second, we were able to take the time to face the front – instead of constantly watching our backs – and observe what's really going on around us, switching off the noise that is coming at us from all directions, we could start to unlock our intuition and listen to our 'true self'.

Walking outside in nature places you in a peaceful and calm environment where you can begin to filter purposeful thought processes from purposeless ones. Your 'true' (or 'authentic') self is the one that cuts through all that's going on around you (including other people's opinions of and attitudes towards you), steering you towards the decisions which best sustain and nurture you as an individual.

Calm assessment of difficult situations allows the authentic self to develop from one that says, 'I can't' or 'I won't' to one that says, 'I can' and 'I will'. You will know when this shift has happened because you will almost immediately get a sense of the power that can be had when you take responsibility for yourself. It isn't always easy, especially at the beginning of the journey, but wherever possible it should be explored. As with anything worth doing, the more you practise, the better you will become.

This last point is important to understand, acknowledge and keep hold of as you begin Walking Therapy. As you walk, you will listen to the narrative in your head – steadily, and without judgement – and hear what it is telling you, good or bad. Once identified, it is entirely within your power to change it.

Limbering up

But first things first. I want you to diarise the time for a walk. No ifs, buts or excuses; simply look at your schedule for the week ahead and add in *one hour* which you will dedicate to walking. Is an hour too long? I don't think so. Even those with the busiest schedules can spare at least one hour per week in which to take a walk, so put this in your diary or in your online calendar now. It could be a morning, a lunchtime or an evening – the choice is yours, though I find that a morning works best of all because your mind is fresh, and it's a great way to gently limber up your senses for the day ahead.

Done it? Good. You will find that, throughout the course of this book, I will try my best not to be prescriptive, but there are some areas in which a few ground rules are exceptionally helpful. Diarising your walks is one of them. I call it an 'estimable duty' – something you're setting in stone that will benefit you in terms of your self-esteem. It keeps you in touch with your sense of power, especially during times when you might be feeling vulnerable and unsure of what might lie ahead.

Where to go?

Before you head out in a random direction, consider the environment in which you live. Is it urban, suburban or rural? If it's the latter, you won't have any problem finding green space and a footpath through it. If it's urban or suburban, you might think you haven't much access to nature, but let's not forget that a surprising amount of the space in which we live is green. In London alone there are 3,000 parks, 35,000 acres of public green space and an astonishing 8 million trees. So even the most urban of urban dwellers has little or no excuse not to get some grass under their feet.

You don't have to walk solely in nature to profit from walking mindfully – but it does help. So head for some greenery wherever possible, but don't feel you need to wander in the wilderness to benefit. If you commute to work, why not walk part of the way instead? If you leave home an hour earlier, you will still be at work on time. Or you might choose to walk part of the journey home, consciously including a park, a wood or a riverside as part of the route. Exploring a map of your home area is a great idea – it shows you all the nearby green spaces and the footpaths you can use to navigate them.

I walk to work via Regent's Park and, even in the middle of London, I'm slowly walking through the grass, paying attention to how it feels under my feet. I feel human, in touch with the space around me, not at all pressured, not in the firing line. And part of that is about creating the space and time. It takes extreme discipline to not 'do stuff', and even more discipline to carve out time where you will just amble along.

Jerry

A Walking Diary

I've found that clients who keep a Walking Diary can really keep track of the progress they're making. It needn't be comprehensive; just note down the date and time of each walk, where you're going and how you're feeling before you set off. When you've finished walking, jot down how you feel again, and what you observed about yourself and your surroundings on the walk.

Matt, a client, kept a diary during a period of depression, which arose following the break-up of a long-term relationship. Matt's world revolved around his ex-partner, with whom he had a child, and he found it extremely difficult to visualise a life in which they were separated from each other. Here is an extract from his Walking Diary, covering his first day on foot:

7 June

Where I'm walking: local woods.
   For how long? One hour.
   With anyone? Just my dog.

How I'm feeling before I set off: depressed. Long-term stressed/task orientated/micro-managing time/too concerned with the future. Carrying too much stuff, mentally.

How I feel now I've finished: slowing down, pulling back from thoughts about past/future – allowing them in where necessary, but refocusing, if possible, on 'the here and now'. Listening: motorway is close by – an artery of stress – yet far enough away not to care. Back, shoulders aching from walking slowly; feeling tired but strong. Observing the dog allows 'hunting' instinct to surface. Watching its alertness, agility, its response to stimuli (squirrels, etc.). Dog is ten years old, but looks young again.

On the way back, I found a quiet bench and slept on it for a few moments. A song was stuck in my head; the Rolling Stones' 'Beast of Burden'. When I woke up, it was to a word I 'heard': 'devolve'.

Making a note of how you're feeling *before* you set off immediately puts you into a state of preparation and anticipation for the journey ahead. This is important because it begins to engage your focus in doing something 'for you'. Your time is precious, particularly that which you devote to yourself, and preparing for it harnesses the spiritual and psychological aspects of Walking Therapy.

Preparing for your walk is also about you taking control of time and making it *manageable* – as we saw earlier (see p. 25), it is very often a lack of manageability that leads to stress, anxiety, drama and chaos. These seemingly small acts of preparation, before you've even taken a step, are helping you to understand how important your management of and responsibility for your time really is.

How to walk

Obvious, right? You just put one foot in front of another and start moving. Well, not quite.

Remember that this is your first venture into Walking Therapy. You've chosen to work on the parts of yourself that feel anxious, vulnerable, despondent, depressed or stressed. These internal aspects are very likely to have external manifestations in that you might move slowly or heavily, your eyes cast down and your shoulders sagging, like you have a weight on them.

This sensation of being burdened isn't going to disappear immediately, but we can do something about making the weight more bearable. So instead of walking with your head down, be aware of your posture, straighten yourself up and walk with purpose and confidence. Try just five or ten minutes of walking confidently – even if you know you're 'pretending' – and see how it feels. You might know this as 'fake it to make it', but it is derived from the 'Pygmalion effect' which we will look at later in the book (see p. 103). For now, all you need to know is that it works.

By using a strong walking posture, you are retraining your brain to 'tell' your body to be more decisive and powerful in your physical movement. Being more decisive, in turn, encourages a greater feeling of self-assurance, which increases confidence levels. Every action you take affects your neural network, so this is a great exercise to start positively reinforcing new behaviour.

Walking this way also helps you to turn negative into positive energy. And not just in the short term, either. And this, over time, will make you more confident and assertive in any future decision-making process you must face, reducing anxiety and procrastination.

But at this stage, let's just concentrate on enabling you to feel good for the hour you are walking. Here are some more suggestions for ways you can walk more confidently:

- **Power striding:** take strong, confident and powerful strides while maintaining a slightly faster pace, swinging your arms back and forth to match your stride. Make sure your feet 'stamp' with each step, as this will connect you to the ground and will help to channel out negative energy. Doing this helps to reduce stress and cortisol levels.

- **Power posture:** rolling your shoulders back and keeping your head up will straighten your posture and improve your core strength and balance. Maintaining a good pace and stride pattern will increase your endurance and stamina over time. After a walk of between thirty and sixty minutes you will feel the positive effects of this exercise – so imagine how you'll feel if you do it three times a week.

- **Power imagery:** creating powerful images and using your imagination as you walk can be a very useful tool and ally. Permit your mind the space to roam freely and access the creative part of your psyche. If animals allow themselves to wander, observe and dream, then so must we. When I was younger, I used to pretend I was a giant leaping from one country to another across the paving stones outside my house. Utilising your imagination in this way, especially if you hark back to childhood, creates the motivation and space to be light-hearted and escapist.

Notice how the three core elements – the psychological, physiological and spiritual (see p. 22) – that are central to Walking Therapy work together in the above exercises. By striding out, you are physically increasing your strength and channelling out stressful negative energies, while your brain is psychologically sending out signals and producing the necessary neurochemicals that are already taking effect, allowing you to feel a bit more confident and assertive within yourself. And the very act of feeling the ground underfoot with every stride is spiritually connecting you to the earth and to nature – the universal parent.

Leave your tech behind

I make no judgement of the fact that we all carry our phones everywhere we go, myself included. The question is, do we leave them on while we walk? And should we listen to music/podcasts/relaxation sessions through our headphones as we're walking? My advice would be to keep the tech at home wherever possible – or at least keep it switched off.

The primary aim of Walking Therapy is to establish a healing connection to nature. If you're listening to music or keeping an eye on your phone or social media, your train of meditative thought is, at the very least, going to be interrupted. This is particularly important in green spaces, where the sounds you need as part of your healing process are all around you – so tune into them instead. Someone calling you, asking if you can do this, that or the other, during your walk is not useful.

The situation is a little trickier in the city, where noise from traffic, construction work and even passing conversations can interfere with your ability to connect almost before you've left home. If you can screen these distractions out naturally, all well and good. If you find they're causing problems, then, by all means, use headphones and meditative music, remembering that the primary connection is between you and the earth. Try to mute the 'phone' part of your mobile and ignore social media if you can. It's a case of common sense and acknowledging that this is your time, for yourself and not to be shared or encroached upon by others. (See Chapter 4 for more on technology.)

EXERCISE: OUR FIRST WALK

This is our first walk together and I want to keep it simple and manageable. You know what kind of schedule you're on in terms of how long you can walk, so make sure you're fully prepared for the journey ahead – check the weather, choose your route and turn off your phone.

Before you set off, just take five minutes to check in with how you're feeling, both in general (for example, stressed/anxious/tired/fraught/frazzled) and about the walk specifically. You don't need to say what you hope to get out of it – it's the journey that counts, not the destination. Use your Walking Diary or the space below to jot down your feelings:

Before I set off I'm feeling:

* ....
* ....
* ....

For the purposes of this particular exercise, it's vital you keep a slow and steady pace and, at the same time (as described above – see p. 34), try to walk purposefully, even if you're not feeling in such good emotional shape: head up, shoulders back, like you're taking back at least some of the power you've been giving away so freely.

For the moment, I'm not asking you to mull over your problems and scramble for solutions. First, you must establish good walking practice and learn how to be mindful of your surroundings. Don't consciously push unpleasant thoughts away; instead, let them in and allow them to pass while refocusing on what you're seeing and hearing *in the present*. Keep a good pace and be observant. Look at your environment with new eyes. Consider:

- how many trees or birds you can name
- if it's a cold/warm/wet/windy day and how these elements make you feel
- what you notice that you haven't noticed previously if you've walked this way before
- the most intriguing aspects of this environment if you haven't been here before
- how it feels *not* to be overstimulated by your phone constantly pinging and bleeping
- what the relative silence around you feels like if you're in deep greenery
- how you respond to noisier surroundings if you're in an urban or suburban environment.

At some point during the walk, and when you feel ready, experiment with speeding up and slowing down. Notice how the change of pace makes you feel. When you walk quickly, you're often channelling anger and stress. When you slow down, you allow yourself to relax, breathe and step out of the tunnel vision of your frantic day-to-day life, raising your eyes up to the trees and the sky to see a broader perspective and get closer to your feelings.

During the final ten minutes of your walk, note how the things you named made you feel – happy, sad, anxious, elated, intrigued . . . You might want to slow right down now, or even sit for a couple of minutes, while you record your observations:

During my walk I experienced:

- ....
  ....
- ....
  ....
- ....
  ....
- ....
  ....

When I experienced the above, it made me feel:

- ....
  ....
- ....
  ....
- ....
  ....
- ....
  ....

Now, continue your walk until your allocated time is up. When you're done, take another quick break and jot down how the walk has made you feel as a whole:

How I feel now I've finished:

- ....
  ....
- ....
  ....
- ....
  ....

Hopefully, you'll feel that the walk has had some benefit for body and mind. Just the fact that you have undertaken it in the first place is a positive step in the right direction. What you have taken away from it, in terms of your reflections listed above, can be packed up and carried forward into your next session. Before you move on to the next chapter, please try this several times and note the differences in your feelings and emotions.

Now let's hear from Ryan, who came to me with a range of issues stemming from work stress to bereavement and divorce. In addition, he was questioning his sexuality. In short, Ryan had lost sight of himself, and when it became obvious he wasn't finding face-to-face sessions entirely comfortable I suggested we tried Walking Therapy. These are some of his reflections on the early stages of the process:

> In a way, the walking was like an uncoiling. I was
> incredibly wound up and walking just helped; the
> physical activity and doing something that felt
> very positive. And that the time was my time. I
> knew I was totally committed to it. It became a
> very positive routine, a ritual. There was natural

silence as well, whereas in a room, if there's a
void, you feel you have to fill it. In the open air,
you notice the sky and the views, and it allows for
a different kind of pace. There is a skill to it and
how that is managed. The pace of it is critical.
Ryan

It may take a few walks to become accustomed to your feelings. But have no doubt: with every step you take, you're doing something different in your life and, therefore, changing your behaviour and thought processes. After all, engaging in Walking Therapy requires commitment and action. And now that your journey has officially begun, it gets even better from this point.

CHAPTER 3: THE SHAME AND BURNOUT CYCLE

Shame is a soul-eating emotion.
Carl Gustav Jung, psychiatrist and psychoanalyst

Hopefully, by now you've walked several times and have kept a log of your observations while outdoors. (Each walk should be at least thirty to sixty minutes, repeated three times per week.) Maybe you've noticed that you've arrived at your destination (work, home or back where you started if you've walked a circular route) feeling generally a little more positive and better prepared for whatever the rest of the day brings.

It's very probable that you've been thinking about your situation: how you arrived at the point you're at and what you would like to happen so that you are no longer having to deal with difficult issues. The walking you've done so far might have moved these issues closer to the surface, as walking in nature is a channel for bringing difficult emotions to light. As we've seen, the release of oxytocin and endorphins as you walk helps you to relax, think about and process such emotions. And maybe you've noticed that you're generally feeling more emotional, or that while walking you've had the occasional 'flash' of clarity about yourself and your situation. If so, that's great. This proves that what you're doing is beginning to work.

Walking is a vehicle to be able to listen to your 'inner voice'. Listening to this voice, observing your intuitive thoughts and trusting in them isn't always easy, especially when there is so much external 'noise' to deal with each day. Yet by not listening to it and choosing to ignore your intuition you are unwittingly abandoning yourself.

If you think to yourself, 'I'd love to go to the cinema (or go for a swim, or meet a friend, or whatever!) but I can't because of all the extra work on my plate this evening', you've just rejected the part of yourself that feels worthy and is seeking to maintain self-worth. When you start to become more aware of all the times you abandon the part of you that deems itself worthy, shunning its desire for self-care, you will quickly notice its retaliation: sadness, anger and general unhappiness.

Let's talk about shame

Like humans, the wolf can experience shame if its environment impacts upon it negatively or it has been rejected by its pack. But in truth, wolves generally work and live together in a supportive environment, and there is a lot we can learn from this type of behaviour.

'Shame' is a hot and much-discussed topic in therapy and self-help, but I find that often people don't really know what it is or understand it – mainly because they are unaware that they are being, or have been, shamed.

Shame takes the form of a critical, negative voice that is constantly interrupting you, putting you down, making you feel small and inadequate, and will inevitably drive you on to act in ways that are detrimental to your health and well-being, until you're at the point of burnout. If your self-talk goes something like, 'You don't deserve to have a rest. You haven't finished what you've said you were going to do, and you need to work harder. I can't believe it takes you this long to complete a simple task . . . what's wrong with you?' you are shaming yourself without knowing it.

When I was a child, I felt stupid and ashamed because I wasn't as academic as the rest of my family. I came to believe that I *was* stupid, which caused me immense difficulties at school. I fell behind badly and didn't have the voice to be able to ask for help. I hoped my parents would pick up on the problems I was having with schoolwork and bullies, but they didn't (they had their own difficulties during this time) and so my concerns went unheard and I felt completely trapped and alone, too scared to verbalise my feelings, fearing that they wouldn't be heeded or considered. And from then on, for me the world didn't feel a safe place to be. It was only when I joined a band, and got into drink and drugs, that I found an escape route, albeit a very unhealthy one.

The dark power of shame

You would never stand over a child and say, 'You're so stupid; no, you can't go out and play, you must do better and then – only then – will I love you.' Yet, you allow your inner 'critical parent' to speak to your 'inner child' in this way. You hear this critical voice and because you are sensitive (and I believe sensitivity lies at the heart of shaming), you act upon it, looking for affirmation from others that you are 'bad', 'not good enough', 'unworthy' and 'need to do better'.

When you shame yourself, you sabotage and abandon your true potential and self-worth out of:

- fear of rejection
- fear of failure
- fear of being exposed as a fraud.

In short, you are afraid of being seen as not 'good enough'.

If you, perhaps, grew up in an environment that was either psychologically or emotionally abusive, you may internalise how you were spoken to in childhood; this then becomes your own inner critical voice and is often carried into adulthood. Or if you were ignored or overlooked as a child, you may have grown up feeling that perhaps you don't matter or are 'unlovable'. Shaming yourself brings with it an innate fear of being rejected and being seen as 'less than' by society. You feel you cannot control other people's reactions towards you, so subconsciously reject and shame yourself first, before someone else can do so, in an attempt to regain a sense of control. Even if this is to the detriment of your own mental health.

You'll see how a vicious circle develops from this. The louder the 'shaming voice', the harder you drive yourself to comply with it. You lose all empathy for yourself because you don't feel worthy enough to receive it. You are no longer connected to what is important and vital for you. And it may be the case that the impossibly high standards you're setting for yourself are reflected in the fact that you're consciously or subconsciously shaming others close to you, either at work or home.

In so-called 'shame societies' such as Japan, where control is maintained and reinforced within an environment of continual guilt, the suicide rate, especially among working-age males, is far higher than it is in many other countries. The West isn't quite there yet (although it is on the increase), but there is no doubt that shame, and what I call 'hierarchical shame' in the workplace, is a big factor for those who overwork and place themselves under the immense pressure that eventually leads to burnout.

The shame–guilt–anger triangle

Those who experience shame usually experience guilt and

anger too. This is predominantly internalised and directed towards themselves, but during times of considerable stress, they may find themselves shunning, belittling or shouting at others as a way of externalising their frustration and making themselves feel more empowered. An example of a shaming inner narrative would be: 'If you don't stay late and get this work done, you're going to look like a total loser in front of everyone, and everyone will then see how incapable you are.' Here we see the triangle at work. The guilt, fear of failure, along with the fear of potentially letting everyone down may also encourage them to overcompensate by working ridiculous hours that extend late into the evening and over the weekend.

I have seen with clients over the years that this is an extremely common recipe for the development of work stress and burnout. At whatever level, burnout is insidious in the way it creeps up. Frequently, I've had clients suffering from burnout who are constantly in tears yet can't understand why. I tell them that when we cry it is not always because we are sad. We also cry when we internalise or repress feelings of anger and frustration, or if we feel tormented by our inability to convey and put into words difficult emotions we are feeling. The more internal anger starts to build, responding and reacting to our own relentless shaming inner narra-tive, the more adrenalin and cortisol are increased and released into the body. And when our adrenal glands become fatigued, we feel totally depleted. *This is burnout.* Here, we can see clearly the relationship between shame and burnout and what it can do if it goes unchallenged and untreated. And it is often our pride that prevents us from asking for help, for fear of being seen as incapable, leaving us feeling still more alone, ashamed and isolated.

Beverley, who we met in the first chapter, was experiencing problems around the fact that while she cared deeply for others, feeling she couldn't let anyone down, she had little or no concept of 'self-care'. Constantly prioritising others before yourself in this way, decreasing self-care and an inability to say 'No' in order to maintain professional boundaries and ethical standards at work are all symptoms of burnout. People often feel completely trapped, along with an increasing sense of responsibility towards others, convincing themselves that if they don't do what is asked of them, everything will fall apart.

In organisations such as the NHS where Beverley works, the caring natures of healthcare workers and their passion for their jobs are often taken advantage of. Ever-decreasing numbers of staff and increased workloads mean that if they're already in the middle of burnout, it just becomes harder and harder to say 'No'. Especially knowing that people's lives may be at stake.

I want to help people and I know I have the skills to make things better for them. I work with families and children, trying to make big crises smoother and better. So I give, give, give. I don't do it for thanks, but people always want more.

I felt very duty-bound, and I loved my young team. I felt totally responsible because I felt I should protect them from all the stuff going on. It sounds like I am a martyr but that's what it was.

Beverley

Beverley's response to ever-increasing pressure on her from senior management was to put still more on herself. She had no idea how to say 'No'. Just getting her to clear a space in her diary for our Walking Therapy appointments was an effort:

*I had an appointment (with Jonathan) and had
to get across town and be there on time. That
was a massive thing because it meant I had to
leave work on time. Yet just doing that broke
that cycle and I still try to use that now, when
there is something I have to leave on time for.
It gave me a focus and some me-time.*
Beverley

As we've learned, Katrina came from a background of family
pressure to 'do well':

*I was the first person in family to go to university
and I felt it was my responsibility to my parents to
'pay them back'. I was living my life for them, not
for myself. Before I left the job I was in, I had forty
people working for me and they all relied on me. I
felt a sense of responsibility to my team, rather
than to the business as a whole. I was always last.
Which is something I still struggle with, if I'm
honest. Before, I wouldn't recognise it when it was
happening, but now I can see when I'm slipping –
maybe eating or drinking too much – and I have a
word with myself and steer my way out of it.*
Katrina

At first, Katrina wasn't keen to open up, even as we were walking.
She questioned why we had 'to go over all this again'. But as
time went on, she understood through Walking Therapy that
from a young age she had prioritised her work above herself.
Her need to be in control at all times was increased by a lack
of trust that if she were to 'let go' of her responsibilities, there

would be anyone capable enough to support her or take over the mantle. And perhaps the motivation to not let go of the role she was now accustomed to was also a way of avoiding a fear of failure, letting others down and the feelings of guilt and shame that would accompany no longer being the dutiful daughter, sister, manager and provider. I also think the prospect of not being in a leadership role increased her fear of no longer receiving love and respect she so desperately sought from others.

I think I am a control freak as well. In most ways! I really struggle with it. Professionally, I have to remember not to lead all the time and let people develop, not do things for them. And in my personal life too. I need to have a plan. That has made relationships difficult. All I really want is someone to look after me, but I can't let go and let them do that.
Katrina

It perhaps goes without saying that my clients are aware they're unhappy, stressed or depressed. By and large they are highly sensitive people, and many of them are tied into the idea that their worlds will collapse if they do something out of the ordinary or say 'No' to whoever or whatever is causing them shame. Even though they know their bodies are under stress and they're feeling dreadful, they feel anxious about making changes. The inner child is crying and saying, 'I want to stop this', but is being ignored, in favour of the inner critical parent who says, 'You must push on, regardless'.

Refiling feelings

Ironically, the more burnt out we feel, the more we seem to accommodate extra responsibility:

*In my work I was very committed to what I did but
I felt overwhelmed and carried on working
through that. I didn't seek help or tell anyone,
until I had to take some time out, which shifted
the balance of things.*

*I'd got to the stage where I'd lost sight of myself. I
was doing a lot of caring for my parents. They both
had illnesses very late in life and needed a lot of
support. And I was bringing up my own children and
getting through a divorce. I didn't give myself any
time and so I went into a big black hole.*

*For me, this manifested in a lack of energy,
not sleeping properly, being very distant, not
opening up, drinking heavily, smoking ridiculous
amounts. It all became very unhealthy . . .*

Ryan

. . . and overwhelming, too, especially when the boundaries were being eroded by such pressures.

In the early stages of Walking Therapy, you will be confronted by a whole range of issues, thoughts and feelings which perhaps haven't been aired before or have been pushed aside. If you see these as 'files', you might be aware that if you haven't had time to deal with them, there is very likely to be a build-up of what I call 'emotional backlog'. When you start to walk, you will notice that instead of being 'present', your brain may start 'refiling' the backlog of previously undealt-with emotions. Which is a very good thing.

If possible, try not to overthink what's going on within this process. The act of walking is stimulating the brain into action, so let any thoughts or feelings arise without trying to interpret or question them. Simply allow your thoughts to 'be', as this will help the refiling process. If you think some thoughts and feelings need more of an outlet than others, by all means, write these down in your Walking Diary as they arise, if you find it cathartic. And, over time, you will find that the state of being 'present' will increase vastly as your emotional backlog lessens.

The following exercise will help you to connect with your breathing. By listening to the air flowing in and out of the nose and mouth and aiming to regulate your breathing pattern, you will stimulate and encourage the process of listening and being 'present', where distractions and 'noise' are at an absolute minimum. This is a great exercise for those who are feeling burnt out and stressed. When you are anxious or stressed you tend to take shallow breaths and, if this continues, you will hyperventilate eventually, putting your body under even more stress. This exercise is specifically focused on breathing out your stresses, frustrations and annoyances while you walk, calming down your body and brain and helping you to 'self-regulate' your breathing pattern. My opera-singer mother taught me how to connect with my diaphragm when inhaling and exhaling, and the importance of supporting your breathing this way.

EXERCISE: WALKING AND BREATHING

Try this exercise in an area of quiet woodland, away from main roads, if you can. Taking a path through the trees will allow you to experience the unique calming quality that being under a natural canopy provides. If this isn't possible, a quiet space in the open air and the natural elements with few distractions should work.

When you arrive at the start of your walk, take a minute or two to notice how you're feeling. If you're keeping a Walking Diary, write these feelings down. Next, take another minute or two to connect with your surroundings. What time of year is it? How does the current season make you feel? If it's damp and cold, do you feel pessimistic? If it's sunny and warm, are you on a natural high?

1. Start your walk and take one short breath in through your nose, lasting no longer than two seconds. Then breathe out of your mouth for about four seconds. Try this a few times to get used to the pattern.
2. Next, imagine yourself breathing in fresh, vibrant and clean energy for two seconds. As you exhale, imagine breathing out a stream of all your stresses, frustrations and negative energies. Again, repeat this several times.
3. Next, try to notice a specific scent around you. As you inhale, try to see a colour in your mind's eye that complements this scent.
4. Now, ask yourself, 'What does this colour remind me of?' and 'How does it represent an aspect of how I currently see myself?' (For example, on a recent walk I breathed in and suddenly detected the aroma of blossom. It made me think of the colour pink, which I associate with healing.)
5. Isolate the words the scent brings up for you (mine being 'healing') and ask yourself, 'Do I need more of this in my life and if so, why has it been lacking?'
6. Take the next few minutes to consciously explore your answers to the questions above. Don't overthink your responses.

Repeat this whole exercise several times during your walk and notice how placing a colour next to a scent helps the brain escape into a more mindful space. When you've finished your walk, take a minute or two to reflect on what you've felt and thought and, if possible, write down the results in your Walking Diary.

Remember: you are not here to 'solve' your difficulties but instead to see them for what they are. Remember also that your brain is consciously working to refile what has been built up, so allow yourself to walk alongside your thoughts and feelings without judgement.

At times, it is almost impossible to vocalise and make explicit the shaming voice inside our heads. This is because we tend to hide shameful feelings and thoughts at all costs. The antidote to shame is to reveal how we truly feel to ourselves and to others, where appropriate to do so.

EXERCISE: WALKING WITH INNER SHAME

This exercise is designed to help you challenge your inner critical parent and to replace it with something more nurturing.

1. Write down the dialogue between your inner critical parent and inner child. For example:
   Inner critic: Look at yourself, you look tired and pathetic. You're such a loser and so weak. You need to toughen up and start doing your job.
   Inner child: I know I look like absolute shit. I'm so

tired. What's wrong with me? No one else looks as tired as I do. You're right, I am such a loser. Maybe I should just quit. But that thought makes me even more stressed and scared.

2. Now take a walk. At the end of the walk have a look at this conversation and respond with a more nurturing dialogue that isn't shaming the inner child. For example:

Nurturing parent: It's hardly surprising as you've been made to work late every day this week and you're doing twice the workload you were contracted to do. When you're feeling tired like this it's so much harder to say 'No' when something is unmanageable. But that is what you need to do. It's not because you're incapable; you just need to take some time off to recover and be gentler on yourself. You can't 'assume' how people feel; some hide it better than others. So just focus on yourself for now.

Learning how to create a more positively affirming inner dialogue will help you to lower your stress levels and provide you with more clarity over time. This exercise gives you an extremely powerful tool that can be used as often as you need it. Remember, as cortisol levels are lowered your personal clarity will increase. Over time, this exercise will help to silence your shaming voice by giving you the opportunity to see your inner dialogue written down in black and white, allowing you to shine some light on the problem, instead of it being left to fester away in the cold, dark recesses of your mind.

Tianna's walk towards the light

Tianna sought my help because she was stressed at work and battling grief following the death of a close friend. At first, she found it hard to make the connection between 'getting better' (as she put it) and walking. The constant pressure of deadlines had taken its toll over the years and Tianna considered making time for herself pointless and difficult. Unhappiness had chipped away at her over time, to the extent that her relationship had ended, and she was regarded as a 'grouch' by her work colleagues.

Our walk begins one early summer's morning in a wood that is partly wild and partly forested with pine trees. We set out from the sunnier part of the wood. 'I'm not so keen on woods,' Tianna admits. 'They're dark, dank places and easy to get lost in.' Although she is aware she has difficulties she would like to solve, Tianna finds it hard to step away from a position of certainty about most things – woods included. I point out that areas heavily populated by trees can be comforting in a very primal sense. Our ancestors knew they were places of shelter and safety.

'But places of danger too,' Tianna says. 'You could be robbed or killed by wild animals.'

'Or you could learn from the wildness,' I reply, 'and embrace uncertainty. You could wander off the path and get lost; equally, you could find something amazing that you didn't know you were looking for.'

We push on into a darker part of the forest. The air here is cooler, stiller. Birds flit between branches almost as shadows and the tall trees seem to amplify the crunch of our footsteps as we walk on paths strewn with fallen pine needles. I notice Tianna has become quieter as we've entered this part of the wood and I judge that the moment might be right to try the Walking and Breathing exercise.

We spend about ten minutes trying this, but Tianna is struggling. 'I just can't smell anything unusual,' she admits. 'Nothing's standing out for me at all. There are no connections between me and anything here.'

Suddenly, Tianna looks very sad. After a minute or so in silence, she speaks again. 'When I was a kid, I played in woods like this all the time,' she says. 'I guess I just grew up and forgot about it. I've lost all those links to the past.'

We walk on anyway, just taking in the sound of the wind whispering at the tops of the pines and feeling the coolness of the forest on our bare arms. Then Tianna stops and bends down to pick up something from the path. She holds it up for me to see. It's a bird's feather, blueish-black in colour.

'It's from a jay,' Tianna tells me. 'They're common in woods like this.' She places the feather next to her cheek and then looks at it intently. 'I love the texture and unique artistry of feathers,' she says. 'This really takes me back.'

'To what?'

'To being a kid. I knew the names of so many birds then. I loved watching them. And collecting their feathers. I used to wish I could make them into quill pens, so I could write with them. Actually – I know what feathers remind me of: ink. They remind me of wanting to write with a quill pen and ink.'

'Why is that important to you?' I ask.

'I always wanted to write,' Tianna says. 'I always thought I had something to say. When I wrote, I felt I was in such a natural place, you know? I could spend hours writing dialogue, descriptions, bits of poetry.'

'So what happened?'

'A science teacher at school discovered my secret scribblings in the back of my exercise book and decided to read them out to the rest of the class. "Our little Shakespeare," he called me. I felt such an idiot!'

Tianna laughs in an attempt to make light of what must have been a mortifying experience. Then she looks disconsolate. Shaming someone in this way can lead to a lifetime of self-doubt and inhibition, which the 'shamed' person may not recognise as coming from that event.

'I never really wrote again after that,' she says. 'Every time I tried, I heard that teacher mocking my efforts. In the end, I gave up completely. Didn't write another word.'

'Do you think you could control that critical voice enough now to have another attempt?'

'I don't know,' Tianna replies, looking optimistic for the first time in weeks. 'What do you think?'

From this point onwards, Tianna and I worked on her recognition of her 'shaming' experience and the critical voice which cut so much happiness and creativity out of her life.

By making connections with seemingly random things (smells, colours, textures, the feel and intricacies of certain objects) we can begin to build associations that were perhaps important to us but have been lost to time or to the shaming 'inner critical parent' that stifles personal growth. Walking mindfully outdoors stimulates our senses, creating associations that may have lain dormant but are still intrinsically part of who we are. Keep trying the 'Walking and Breathing' exercise and listen carefully to what nature is telling you. You might be surprised by what you discover.

Jerry gradually realised that by slowing down, he began to reconnect with all that was around him:

When I walk to listen to myself, I slow way down and as soon as I go from commute speed, Speed C, and slow down to Speed A (ambling), my mood state changes immediately. It's like being younger – like when you walked to school – you're not squeezed for time. Slowing down feels like time-travelling. The experience of slow ambling is so unusual that it calls to mind experiences from thirty or forty years ago in the sense of being a child, having time, being able to look around and notice the flowers that had the sweet stems on them. That's not something that I've done for decades because I'm too busy turning every experience into a competition.

Jerry

When you feel burnt out, the world is a blur and you disconnect from your surroundings. You observe nothing, you feel nothing but torment and shame for feeling this way and your pride takes a major hit. But you are a worthy individual, so try to focus on the value that you bring to the world, not what has been stripped away by feeling stressed all the time. You deserve better than the fast-paced, stress-filled life you have designed for yourself.

The process of regularly taking time out of your day to venture outside reminds you that you are human and not alone in this world. If you slow down, you will see what has been right in front of you: that life has and always will be there waiting for you when you choose to connect with it. Trust in this process and I promise the answers you seek will slowly start to present themselves over the course of time.

CHAPTER 4: THE GIVING AND
TAKING OF POWER

'No' is a complete sentence.
Anne Lamott, American author, in *Operating Instructions:*
A Journal of My Son's First Year

When we consider the wolf, we think of it as a truly wild creature, respecting no physical boundaries or frontiers that might restrict its innate desire to roam freely. The truth, of course, is more complex than that. Wolves exist in closely ordered packs, in which hierarchies are firmly established and clear boundaries set. Such boundaries, particularly between males and females and what we might describe as 'alpha wolves' and those lower down the pack's social pecking order, are vital to its structure and functionality. If they break down, the pack becomes vulnerable to starvation and attacks from other packs. In short, the absence of boundaries will threaten its survival.

In this chapter, we will be looking at the importance of boundary-setting for us as humans. And while I don't expect you to snap wolfishly at those who challenge your boundaries (though you might!), there are sophisticated ways in which you can establish and protect them through the work we will do together, and not feel guilty about it.

Setting boundaries and sticking to them is a fundamental

part of human existence. How do you feel when someone you don't know (or have only just met) stands too close to you, talking right into your face? What is it like when someone outstays their welcome, borrows something without asking or becomes overly intrusive and passive-aggressive in the way they communicate with you on a daily basis?

Generally, we are clear about how we feel when this happens, and we expect other people to abide by such 'rules'. But the person who loses the ability to maintain and uphold personal and professional boundaries will rapidly lose sight of what their personal limitations are and will no longer be able to manage their emotions or workload. Clarity of thought and the ability to make good decisions for our personal health fall by the wayside, along with our confidence and integrity. Therefore, we need to be able to understand what our personal limitations should be in order to achieve a healthy life/work balance. It is imperative that we recognise and connect with the necessity of putting boundaries in place at all times.

Why boundaries are breached

We are all guilty of letting boundaries drop (or not establishing them at all) when we feel sufficiently pressured into submission. For example: we've already put in a ten-hour day at work (without extra pay) and now the boss is asking if we can stay on another couple of hours just to finish some paperwork. It's the last thing we want to do, but we do it anyway. Or we take work home at weekends because 'otherwise, I'll be chasing my tail next week'. Or we'd rather have a quiet night in, but choose to stay out late in the pub because 'that's what everyone else is doing tonight'. All these scenarios can mean that we sacrifice time we set aside for ourselves.

Saying 'Yes' to requests for our time can be life-enhancing if they benefit us, but equally, there must be times when we say 'No' and mean it. We are all aware of the terms 'yes-man' or 'people-pleaser' and the connotations of subservience and gullibility they carry – but even so, we still very often say 'Yes' when 'No' would be more appropriate.

Why do we do this? Because we want to be liked, and to be thought of as a 'good person'. At the root of 'people-pleasing' is fear – the fear of others' opinions of us, the fear of being fired, the fear of confrontation or the fear of standing out and being shamed by those around us or being seen as a 'pariah'. We don't like letting people down and being the cause of disappointment. To do so leaves us feeling guilty and ashamed that we 'should' or 'could' have done what was asked of us. We don't want to be thought of as 'selfish', so we constantly put ourselves last. And when we do this, we leave ourselves vulnerable to the demands of others and under increasing pressure to go the extra mile, even if it's at considerable personal cost. Before we know it, we have slipped into what I call 'emotional overdraft'. This is where we tend to give more and more of ourselves to others, leaving nothing to sustain our own emotional well-being. We strive to meet demands out of a desperate need to people-please and eradicate our feelings of guilt in the process. Almost immediately, we resent the other person for asking us in the first place, when in truth, we are angry at ourselves for being unable to say 'No'. Why? Because we had nothing to give in the first place and now feel even deeper in emotional overdraft, perpetuating the cycle of shame and self-criticism.

Those who do prioritise their well-being, on the other hand, are in emotional credit because they are able to set adequate personal boundaries for themselves and don't feel resentment as they can give freely at no cost to their mental health or well-being.

Is the desire to be 'liked' worth sacrificing your happiness for, or a reasonable excuse to open yourself up to huge amounts of stress and regret? Are the detrimental effects that stress is having on your mind, body and spirit as a result of 'people-pleasing' a justifiable price to pay for being able to declare that you're 'never selfish'?

As I said in the Introduction, the worst trauma occurs not when we're abandoned by others, but when we abandon ourselves, and it's worth reinforcing this in the context of boundary-setting. If you cannot set boundaries and you say 'Yes' to everything – even when your intuition is screaming 'No!' – then you're abandoning yourself by not remaining true to what the authentic part of your being is trying to tell you.

Managers and HR people who face their own stresses and pressures are not adequately enforcing break-times and reasonable working hours in the mistaken belief that it's more important to be 'seen' to be busy, regardless of whether one is actually being productive or not. This leadership style or belief system is out of date and out of keeping with current approaches to mental health within an organisation. So it's all the more encouraging to see that companies that do embrace flexible working hours and integrate well-being programmes are already seeing positive changes within their teams, contributing towards staff retention rates.

This is why you need to be in charge of creating and setting your own personal boundaries – by scheduling adequate breaks for yourself throughout the day, for example. Waiting for someone else to enforce these boundaries on your behalf, such as your boss, is not the way forward and will not fill you with a feeling of empowerment. In fact, it is the opposite and means handing over your power.

WALK WITH YOUR WOLF

Your power is only ever yours to give away

The potential fallout from having handed over your power is
even more inner turmoil, chaos, anxiety and stress, along
with increased feelings of powerlessness, vulnerability and low
self-esteem. Waiting or relying on others to make us aware of
what our boundaries 'should' be is futile. Make no mistake,
you and you alone must take full responsibility and accountability for your actions, which includes establishing strong
and clear personal boundaries for yourself.

In short, if you remain a 'people-pleaser' and your main
objective is to be 'liked' by others, you will *lose* your objectivity,
integrity, authenticity and sense of empowerment to be 'unique'
and 'different'.

But there is another road ahead that doesn't involve
plummeting into the depths of despair in which you no longer
feel you have a sense of autonomy. You have a right to your
autonomy – as do all of us – and you need to exercise
your right to be this way. Learning to stand up for yourself
is evidence that you are starting to reclaim your power once
again.

So let's begin by identifying where a boundary has been
breached for you on more than one occasion. Think of a
time, or several times, when you said 'Yes' but really wanted
to say 'No'.

I say 'Yes' instead of 'No' when:

- ....
- ....
- ....

Now, ask yourself why you feel you can't say 'No'.

I can't say 'No' in this situation because:

- ....
- ....
- ....

Lastly, ask yourself what might happen if you did say 'No'? What's the absolute worse-case scenario here? For example, if you told your boss you were no longer working late every night and you were subsequently fired, what might happen next? Could you take the company to tribunal? Could you find a job in a less pressured, more employee-friendly company? Will you be courageous enough to prioritise yourself and your happiness? This might feel like catastrophising, but it is seriously worth some thought. You only have one life, after all.

If I do say 'No', what's the worst that can happen?

- ....
- ....
- ....

And if it does happen, what can I do about it?

- ....
- ....
- ....

By using this questioning 'worse-case-scenario' approach, hopefully you'll see that the perceived difficulties that prevent you from raising boundaries and saying 'No' almost always have solutions. If you're clear and confident about the boundaries you set, and you communicate these in an equally clear, confident and non-confrontational way, you *will* be respected. Even better, if you set clear boundaries at work, you will be much more confident about setting them in your personal life too.

Let me introduce you to Elliot. When we first met, Elliot was taking sick leave from his demanding job. A period of work stress and his descent into heavy drinking had caused a breakdown. Elliot was used to being a problem-solver, a fixer and everyone's rock. He was known as 'Mr Reliable'. We talked face-to-face at my private practice indoors for a considerable time before we decided to use Walking Therapy. Indoor therapy had created a feeling of safety at this point in his therapeutic process, and it took Elliot four sessions to acclimatise to Walking Therapy, but when he did the effect was staggering. It immediately improved his psyche, confidence and overall demeanour. It was clear to see that Elliot's relationship with nature grew when he committed to taking a walk each day and maintained this personal boundary. This simple daily ritual became a vital anchor for him to maintain personal clarity and good mental health, which I'm happy to say is still very much the case today.

*Before I had that breakdown, I always saw myself as
the rock; the person who could be relied on: 'Give
him a shout and he'll sort it out' – that sort of thing. I
got the pleasure in giving, not receiving. Learning not
to be in control and not to be in charge created a*

much calmer and more considered self. Rather than being switched on all the time, ready for action to fix something for someone, after therapy I realised I could happily stand aside, let someone else take the wheel and let them get on with it.

I went back to work eventually, where I was able to put healthy boundaries around myself. I work as a lawyer in New York and London and it can be quite an aggressive, pressured and male-dominated environment. But setting boundaries allowed me to be able to say, 'This is what I can deliver and if it's not good enough, so be it'. And amazingly, people are happy with that. I put my best efforts into my work, but boundaries are in place now. Modern life is twenty-four hours and so Walking Therapy is flying in the face of what's expected, but it's made life so much simpler. Evenings and weekends are now on my terms. I can choose to work them or not. And it's been OK at work.

Elliot

For Elliot, the therapy sessions we had, both inside and outdoors, helped him to achieve a certain security in the decisions he made around boundary-setting:

With boundary-setting, it's all about how you deliver it and put it across. It's like children; if you give them sensible boundaries, they're much happier knowing what those boundaries are. It might not make you popular in the short run, but it's effective in the long run and you gain respect from others and within yourself as well. That's a very important part of it.

Elliot

Switch off to switch on

Let's now take outdoors what we've learned about boundaries.

While you're walking, there are several questions you can ask yourself (in addition to those already addressed above), which can also be carried as part of your 'therapeutic backpack' or 'toolkit'. You can decide on whatever terminology or visual aid works for you. Let's just say these are the tools you will develop to give you more confidence in the face of adversity. The Walking with Boundaries exercise I've devised (see p. 70) will empower you to take personal responsibility for your well-being and address why you need to have boundaries in your life.

We live in an age where technology is commonplace. Everything we need to run our personal and professional lives is within our computers, tablets or phones. And yet, I can't tell you over the years how many clients of mine who work in the city have either dreamed of or enjoyed flying on aeroplanes, as it is a time where most people are forced to stop using their phones or looking at their laptops.

When travelling on the London Underground to my private practice, I noticed that the train had become my office, and I was answering emails, organising my Outlook calendar, taking calls or Photoshopping pictures to post on Facebook or Instagram. Before I even got into work I was overwhelmed and overstimulated. And then I would do the same through my lunch break and on my way home too. Even when socialising with friends, I would find myself looking at emails that would quickly take me back to a place of stress, instantly transporting my brain into an active working mindset and headspace. The more I noticed myself doing it, the more it started to annoy and frustrate me.

One day, I left my phone at home by accident. Then things got really interesting. Suddenly, I connected with everything around me. As my eyes wandered, I witnessed most people looking downwards; not connecting with each other, not observing what was happening in their vicinity and relinquishing the use of their imagination. What most of us don't realise is that we can all suffer very easily from auditory and retinal overstimulation, detrimental to the efficiency of how our brains function, to our central nervous systems and to our bodies as a whole. Such overstimulation (especially from overuse of phones, tablets and laptops) vastly increases the levels of adrenalin and cortisol released into the body as a survival response, and can, over time affect our immune systems. We see children become overstimulated in this way, but for some reason we seem to think we're resistant to it as adults. Which isn't the case at all.

So before we even step out, we can create a personal boundary very easily – by switching off our phones. As useful as they are, and as connected as they make us feel, phones have an insidious way of encroaching upon every corner of our lives, stifling our freedom of thought and taking us away from being truly present with ourselves and others. When they're on, so are we, and the temptation to check them frequently is incredibly hard to resist. It's a habit, like any other, and is something we all need to be more aware of and stricter about.

Let's look at setting that personal boundary right now, by *turning off* your phone for the duration of your walk. Walking without technology – without the distraction of ringtones, bleeps and notifications – and relearning to observe your surroundings, people, colours, sounds and scents helps bring a sense of calm, serenity and fulfilment into your life. This, in turn, is essential for self-regulation, processing your thoughts and for daily reflection. It's also essential for your brain to be able to work efficiently and effectively without feeling constantly under duress. This is why ensuring that you're disconnected from technology, and the realm of disruption and drama it can potentially bring you into contact with, is the first boundary you need to put in place for yourself. You may think you're wasting time spent away from your phone, but in fact, you're gaining time. Because while your mind is recovering, you're starting to notice, connect and engage with the world outside once again. It will get easier, and over time, it will feel more comfortable and familiar.

EXERCISE: WALKING WITH BOUNDARIES (AND WITHOUT TECHNOLOGY)

If you stop looking down at your phone and hiding away from the world and instead, start looking up, and reconnect, your world will get a lot bigger very quickly and you perhaps won't feel as isolated or alone.
Without further ado:

1. Before you set off, turn off your phone and put away your laptop.
2. At the start of your walk, close your eyes for a second and observe what you hear around you. Repeat this as many times as you need to, and every time try to listen in more detail.

3. After doing this a few times, walk slowly and observe in detail what you see. If you see a sign hanging from a shop window that is crafted well, admire the craftsmanship, the material it's made from and the year it was probably made. What does it remind you of? Or make you think of?

4. Allow your environment to start stirring your thought processes; relinquish control and see where your subconscious takes you.

5. If your body wants to sit down, trust your intuition. Find a place to sit and reflect. Once again, allow your mind to process certain thoughts. Even if it starts thinking about work, the fact that you're not overstimulating your retinal or auditory senses will help you process these thoughts more effectively.

6. If someone catches your eye on your walk, be sure to make a connection and acknowledge their presence. Notice how this makes you feel.

How did you feel about this exercise and about setting yourself the personal boundary of switching off technology? As I mentioned before, being without technology, even for a short time, can be very stressful for many people. Maybe this is because we are so dependent upon phones and social media for work purposes; but it's also because technology is designed to give us a feeling of pleasure and reward, and to make us feel 'special'. Are we perhaps starting to become more intimate with our phones and technology than we are in the human relationships that surround us daily? Do we invest more time in virtual relationships than real ones? Is our self-worth now being governed by interactions on social media rather than the interpersonal activities that exist outside them? Without knowing it, our reliance upon technology may now have become an unhealthy addiction.

If you notice you're finding it harder to switch off your phone, this is something you need to address. Having your phone taken away from you suddenly may even cause acute separation anxiety. If you're someone who uses their phone a great deal, it's likely you didn't find the exercise easy at all. If so, try it again tomorrow and continue for an hour each day until the anxiety lessens. Cutting down on the 'noise' that technology generates will get easier over time, I promise, and as I've mentioned, it's a really great way of starting to set boundaries for yourself, which we're going to look at now from a slightly different perspective.

Boundary-setting and walking

A boundary has two sides to it: the side you stand behind and the side another person stands behind. It protects you from what others may throw your way and vice versa.

Unfortunately, boundaries can be abused, often by egocentric behaviour, to prove a point or to bully someone into sub-mission. In a hierarchy, this is usually acted out by a person in a place of authority and is technically known as 'an abuse of power'. This is why it is important to always check and ask yourself what motivation is behind the boundary you wish to put into place.

Ultimately, we look for personal boundaries to be fair, placed respectfully and firmly with the clear intention of benefiting our current situation. Victoria's boss stepped over the invisible boundary line time and again, reducing her to tears. Victoria's way of coping was to go out drinking most nights, but this only exacerbated her depression. When she stopped drinking and began to make healthier choices for her evenings, she realised she had to push back on the boundaries her boss was using as bullying tools and set some clear ones of her own.

During our Walking Therapy sessions, Victoria and I worked on designing pre-written scripts that she was eventually able to utilise, so that she wouldn't lose her voice in challenging situations. (I will speak more about this in the next chapter.) The scripts helped her to set and deliver strong, impermeable boundaries that reconnected her with her power and confidence, helping to mediate and control her fight, flight and freeze mechanisms in confrontational situations, and stand her ground when necessary.

My boss was awful, but I couldn't hold my own. She would really offend me, and I would burst into tears. When she talked to me personally, saying negative stuff, I would break down and not be able to be confident. I would walk into her office unprepared, then it would hit me, and my automatic reaction was to cry. I knew it would happen every time.

Jonathan and I worked on setting strong boundaries and on improving my demeanour. And it really worked. That whole power dynamic massively shifted, and I realised that if I was stressed and unhappy, I could just leave the job. Knowing that made me feel more empowered. I learned how to calmly walk into a meeting with her. The difference in me probably shocked her.

I learned to imagine what to expect from her and have a response to it. I had notes in my head. I'd have an answer for what she was coming up with. I now walk into situations way more prepared than I've ever been.
Victoria

On your next walk, ask yourself the following questions (if it's helpful, jot down the answers below or in your Walking Diary):

- Do you see the purpose of physical boundaries and how they may provide you with a feeling of safety and security? Or do you not see their purpose at all?

  ....
  ....

- Do you see a fence or wall as a useful boundary or an unnecessary obstacle? Is the need for one's privacy a blessing or a nuisance?

  ....
  ....

- Do you feel that boundaries are there to be broken, or maintained and looked after?

  ....
  ....

On your walk, make a list of the physical boundaries you see among natural surroundings. These might be a stone wall that protects houses on the shore from the sea, an old fence or rocks that stop you falling off a steep hill or certain types of tree that shelter you from rainfall and provide you with cover. I want you to visually connect and see the purpose of creating and setting boundaries, and to understand that they protect your well-being from many different types of potential threats.

The physical boundaries I've noticed include:

- ....
- ....
- ....
- ....

These boundaries are there to protect:

- ....
- ....
- ....
- ....

Embracing the need for personal boundaries will allow you to clearly communicate your personal limitations, both to yourself and others. This will mean that you can see who does or doesn't respect your well-being, who values your self-worth and who isn't intimidated by your self-confidence. And if you tend to people-please, putting others' needs before your own, a boundary will help to protect and give precedence to your personal needs above and beyond anyone else's. Because if you don't know how to prioritise yourself and fully support your own needs, you cannot expect to support or meet someone else's with any real success. So take a moment in your day to ask yourself: 'When was the last time I truly owned my power, asserted my boundaries and stood up for myself? And what would this look like if I did?'

CHAPTER 5: MAKING NEW STORIES

Givers have to set limits because takers rarely do.
Henry Ford, American industrialist (1863–1947)

As we saw in the previous chapter, setting boundaries for yourself and others is about maintaining self-respect and self-care. It's about taking back your power, being true to yourself and learning to say 'No' when you might normally say 'Yes'.

However, like many things in life, putting theory into practice isn't always easy. We can work on boundary-setting as carefully and calmly as possible when we're in the comfort of our own headspace while out walking, but it's when we step back into the 'real world' (or rather the world we've become accustomed to) that the challenges of boundary-setting, particularly around other people, truly arise.

Today, we're hearing far more about boundary-setting through the media than ever before (for example, the #MeToo movement), yet it is the case that others continue to flout or ignore our boundaries on a daily basis. We tell ourselves that we won't give in to unreasonable demands in the workplace or power struggles in our domestic lives – then, when a boundary-challenging situation arises, we fall at the first hurdle. The temptation to say 'Yes' is overwhelming, particularly if it takes the heat out of a situation, thereby disarming any fear of confrontation, but when this happens, we not only capitulate (again), we hand away our power and repress our anger.

The same is also true when a boundary is challenged and your reaction to that is out of proportion to the challenge itself. We call this 'disproportionate anger'. It's the 'glass-of-water-in-the-face' moment, that sudden split-second impulse to vent your anger. At the time, it might have felt the right thing to do, or perhaps you had no control over your reaction at all, but afterwards you're left with a creeping sense of shame, anxiety and annoyance at yourself that you might have handled the situation better, or at least differently. And that's not to say that such a reaction is always inappropriate – sometimes it's the only reaction to an intimidating, boundary-busting situation. But it is a very definite line in the sand, and once you've crossed it there is no going back.

As I've mentioned, all humans have a stress response commonly known as fight, flight or freeze mode (see p. 17). This happens when we perceive a person, action or situation as a potential threat or danger. It also occurs when we feel tired, exhausted and vulnerable. Animals have the same response too. Look at how the wolf reacts when cornered, its life under threat. Does it roll over on its back, belly in the air, in a gesture of surrender? Or does it fight like everything depends on this moment? While we are not as instinctual as the wolf, and do not have to battle for our sheer survival in the face of imminent death, our response can be somewhere along the same spectrum.

Time for a new story

The stress response can be circumvented by coming up with a different story about what is going on. With preparation and practice, it is possible to put aside the innate, immediate desire to either get angry, roll over or do nothing in favour of a more measured response that is wholly in your favour. The answer to fight, flight or freeze is in the creation of a script – a response to a situation comprised of a pre-prepared, pre-written boundary that you carry in your head and pull out whenever you meet that threat. Designing such a script (which, if it's helpful, can be written down in your Walking Diary and become part of your toolkit) will allow you to keep your 'voice' in any situation and hone the ability to create a personal boundary that makes you feel safe, secure and confident.

We've all had the experience of wishing we could go back in time to a situation where different words or actions might have had a more positive outcome. The phrase 'hindsight is a wonderful thing' is bandied about, mostly in irony, but hindsight is, in fact, a useful tool when planning scripts to be used for similar situations in the future.

Meet Winston.

Winston holds a high-pressured senior position in the creative arts sector. He is in his late forties and increasingly finds himself surrounded by much younger work colleagues who appear to have far more energy, drive and verve than he has. He knows he's a respected senior manager with many achievements under his belt; he is also aware that, in his workplace, creativity is seen as the domain of the young. 'When you're my age, it's assumed you're creatively burnt out,' Winston told me. 'I know my ideas don't come as thick and fast as they once did, but I still feel like I've lots to offer. But no one seems to be listening.'

Winston feels he is being deliberately sidelined, citing the removal of much of his input into a couple of key projects as evidence for this. Yet he did not take this up with his superiors or confront them about his frustrations. Instead, he allowed these disappointments to simmer.

'I got to the point where I was ready to blow,' he said.

We were walking up a steep hill close to Winston's home on the south coast. The day was a blustery one; typical coastal weather involving showers, sunshine, wind and scudding clouds. Conditions were as changeable as Winston's mood as we trudged up the chalk hill. It was clear that he loved the creativity and glamour of his job but felt severely threatened by what he saw as the dominance of the 'kids'.

'There they are, with their social media and other weird obsessions that I don't understand,' he muttered. 'I'm out of touch with them – I know I am. But I'm still good at what I do, and I'm respected in the industry. And no way will I be sidelined.'

As we walked, I noticed Winston occasionally kicking aside twigs and stones. He wasn't doing this consciously, but I detected more than a note of frustration in this action. I asked him what happened when he finally 'boiled over' at work.

'We were in a meeting,' he said, 'and one of the young guys, Fergus, was really holding court with his ideas. He loves the sound of his own voice and no one else could get a word in. I told him to slow down and let other people speak. There was a silence. Then he said something like, "I think you'll find the team's all behind me, Winston, except for you. As ever."

'Well, that was it. I just lost it. I gave it with both barrels. I really ranted, telling him he was arrogant, ignorant, deluded – the lot. No one said a word. They all looked very uncomfortable. I must have gone on for a couple of minutes and at the end of it, when I'd run out of steam, Fergus just smirked at me and said, "OK, whatever".

'The meeting ended pretty soon after that. I took a breather outside and thought about what had just happened. I was trying to convince myself that I was right to let him have it so dramatically. But in my heart, I knew I'd made a fool of myself. Judging by his reaction, though, I assumed he didn't really care about it.

'I was wrong, of course. He went straight to my line manager and said I'd bullied and humiliated him. He was in tears, his colleagues were fluttering all around him – in short, he made a real song and dance about it. That afternoon, I was called in by my manager and given a dressing-down which, although delivered calmly and politely, demolished me very effectively.

'Since then, I know I've been sidelined. A couple of projects I was overseeing were suddenly handed to a colleague and there is a definite "atmosphere" whenever I'm there. It's really doing my head in, and yet I know I'll have to face this situation again sometime – I'm the manager, it's my job to put people in their place when I feel they're out of order.'

As Winston told me this story, his kicking of various objects along the path continued. I pointed it out to him and he winced. 'I know,' he said. 'My anger levels are through the roof. I'm snapping at my partner and our kids. It isn't their fault. They're just in my firing line. I feel all over the place. If only I could turn the clock back . . .'

Obviously, Winston couldn't do that. But as we walked, I suggested that he revisited the scene in the office, recreating it in his mind's eye. This is what I call the Time-Machine Exercise (see p. 83), which involves 'travelling' back to the moment where you wish you'd given a different response and trying to create an alternative script. In a way, it's like reshooting a scene from a film.

Winston asked me to give him a few minutes and he slowed down noticeably. A few specks of rain began to fall as he considered his response. Then he stopped and turned to face me.

'This is how it should've gone,' he said. 'When I intervened, I should've said something like, "These are great contributions, Ferg, but I want to keep this meeting short and so I'll open the discussion to everyone else."

'And if he'd said, "I think everyone's behind me, except for you," I'd have just stayed calm, allowed a moment's silence to enter the room and then said, "That's probably a matter of opinion, Ferg, but I'm happy to talk to you about it after the meeting. In the meantime, guys, shall we continue the discussion?"'

Winston can't do anything to change events in the past, but he now knows he can calmly handle future situations that have potential for trouble, while laying down firm boundaries. And you can learn to do the same. Every time you develop a pre-written script, you will build up a vocabulary of different responses that can be used time and again in the future in a variety of social and work situations. After all, past experience is a chance for self-development, and to ask yourself what you could have said or done differently. As an example, if you're someone who feels panicked in a moment of confrontation, a pre-written script such as, 'I hear what you're saying, but I will need to give that a little more thought' sets a personal boundary and provides you with a much-needed period of time in which to formulate a response that you feel happy with. This method can be applied to many different types of situations. And, importantly, it works.

THE TIME-MACHINE EXERCISE

Now it's your turn. As you walk, think of a situation in which you regret saying or doing something. 'Recast' this event, as though you are a film director who has decided to reshoot a scene. In your mind's eye, run the scene again and introduce in the space provided the dialogue you'd rather have said or the action you wish you'd performed:

With hindsight, I would have said:

....

....

Now look at your new script carefully and imagine deploying it by adapting it to various situations:

When I'm challenged by:

....

I can respond by saying:

....

During our walk, I also introduced Winston to the Alter-Ego Exercise. This can be employed in times where you may find it difficult to access the more confident, wise and powerful part of yourself, especially in challenging situations. A bit of imagination is required for this one, as I want you to select a person – real or fictional – who has inspired you on more than one occasion. It could be anyone who has an air of confidence, calmness and certainty.

THE ALTER-EGO EXERCISE

While you're walking, think of someone who inspires you (famous, not famous, living, dead, friend, relative, stranger, fictional character):

My alter-ego is:

....
....

Now ask this person a few open-ended questions:

- How do you think I handled this situation?
- How could I have handled it better?
- How would you have handled it?
- What might I learn from this for the future?

Try not to pre-empt the conversation, just listen, take note of what your alter-ego is 'saying' and, as you're walking, try to see how their advice might influence your approach next time you face a challenge.

I asked Winston to think of someone who fitted this profile and who might have handled his office argument in a cooler way. Again, he thought for a while before answering. 'Paul McCartney,' he said.

I asked why. 'He's been mega-famous since he was a teenager,' he replied, 'and yet he seems to handle every situation thoughtfully and carefully. No one can be that famous and escape a few arguments – I wouldn't like to have taken on John Lennon – but no matter what's happening, he always seems positive and optimistic.'

I asked Winston what his alter-ego would have done with Fergus, the outspoken employee. 'I think McCartney would've teased him a bit,' he replied, 'but only to lighten the atmosphere. Then he would've praised Fergus's ideas and maybe asked others to comment on them. That might have proved more enlightening in the long run.'

Winston's experience reminded me of a time I struggled with self-confidence when speaking to large groups of people about my therapeutic approach. I found myself talking faster, tripping over my words and becoming very anxious as a result. I needed a template of a person to model myself on to rebuild my confidence. For some reason, the actor Morgan Freeman popped into my head – possibly because of the way he speaks so calmly, never rushing his words, employing a melodic tone of voice and engaging whoever he is talking to, whether in person or on screen.

As Morgan Freeman was floating through my imagination, I decided to have a 'chat' with him, and ask him for some presentation-skills tips. Without trying to pre-determine what he might say, I simply let go and heard him reply: 'Slow down. Don't try too hard. Trust and believe in every word you say and be interested in those words. If you believe it, others will believe it too. For those who want to listen, speak to them. For those who don't . . . well, that's OK also. It's their loss. It's OK to be anxious, because being anxious just means that you care. And if I'm honest, a little anxiety always lends itself to a more emotional performance. So don't worry. Trust in your words and everything else will take care of itself.'

I followed the advice and my next presentation found me much calmer, slower and more reflective. And I got a great reception from the audience. Looking back, I realise that I chose Morgan Freeman because he represented a calmer, wiser part of my alter-ego hidden in the recesses of my subconscious. Winston chose Paul McCartney because he might know how to defuse a situation with humour and be inclusive without letting go of control. In both our alter-egos, the thoughtful part of our psyches was able to provide balance to the more anxious, stressed, 'hair-trigger' parts of ourselves.

Anger is an energy

Winston's use of scripts and the alter-ego exercise was a very useful way of preparing for future situations where boundaries might be challenged or breached, but we still had the problem of finding an outlet for his anger. As he said, his frustrations had not only been demonstrated by an outburst at work, but also by anger issues at home. He felt guilty and ashamed of his behaviour and was obviously fearful that he would continue to be angry, especially around his partner and their children.

The problem with anger is that if it isn't allowed to be expressed externally, it tends to be internalised. And, like a pressure cooker with the lid shut tightly on it, at some stage it will boil over. It needs to find an outlet; after all, as the song says, 'Anger is an energy' (Lydon 1986)[5] and scientifically speaking, energy cannot be destroyed – it needs to go somewhere.

People attempt to supress anger in many ways; often, because they are afraid of what they're feeling, or they're scared of what their anger may do if unleashed. Others feel ashamed of experiencing anger at all, seeing it as unnecessary, ugly and purposeless. However, repressing will simply mean it is suppressed until another time. And, more often than not, it will rear its head via acts of aggressive behaviour, violence and general self-destruction. Over time, repressed anger can turn into anxiety, depression and burnout. Suicide is also common among those who are never able to vocalise their anger, so it's important to learn how to manage these powerful feelings to prevent such long-term destruction.

The spectrum of anger ranges from low-level, such as sulking, petulance and frustration, to more high-level emotions including rebellious anger, rage and murderous rage. If we internalise our anger, it will slowly intensify over time and move from low-level to high-level, eventually manifesting itself in explosive or implosive behaviours.

Generally, people are not good at managing anger or aggression healthily. As a born-and-bred south Londoner, I've become accustomed to using sarcasm as my outlet (which is, essentially, passive-aggression) and on many occasions have offended others without the intention of doing so. My own difficulties with drink and drugs also stemmed from rebellious anger that was never allowed to be expressed openly and honestly. Instead, it came out in addictive behaviour. I didn't attack others; instead, I attacked myself through drinking more and drugging even harder.

Drink and drugs were always a way of kicking the shit out of myself; they were something I had full autonomy over in my life at a time when I felt truly powerless. Ronan O'Rahilly, my manager, understood my anger and encouraged me to express it creatively and safely in a way that I could understand and conceptualise, and that would no longer cause harm to myself or others. Music became my way of channelling what began as essentially negative energy into something coherent, positive and beautiful.

When I first met Beverley, whose journey we have followed in earlier chapters, I was aware that she had unresolved anger issues about her inability to say 'No' to intense pressure at work. As time went on, I realised that her anger was also connected to her upbringing in Zimbabwe and her feelings of being a displaced person (she was forced to leave her country because of the political situation). Yet she had no idea that it is fine to be angry, instead taking on more and more work, which she really resented.

> *During my first Walking Therapy session, one of our primary goals was to be able to express and talk about anxiety and talk about feelings of anger and realise it is OK. We did a lot of work around parent/child roles, when I was acting as child or parent in different situations. The work we did helped me to see where I was taking on these roles with people I worked with and how such roles weren't very helpful. I could be the unforgiving parent who was hard on my inner child, but I could never be the angry kid, shouting back.*
> **Beverley**

Part of the work with Beverley included naming feelings. She found it difficult to understand that she had a right to them. The only place she could feel safe, and express her feelings through crying, was in nature. I encouraged her to use a Walking Diary, where she could name what she was feeling and rate it on a scale of 1 to 10. This worked well for her, and in time she came to realise that it was OK and healthy to express feelings.

I also asked her to download an 'emotional vocabulary chart' that includes different variants of emotions and ways to describe how she might feel on a daily basis, which she also found useful.

I learned how to say 'No' and I can get angry now.

At work, I always felt I had to be happy for everyone all the time. I remember standing up for myself to my boss before she left, and I came bouncing up to Walking Therapy that day because it was the first time I'd said 'No'. I can't remember the exact circumstances, but I do remember that cathartic feeling. Now, if I have a difficult situation, I will take the time to go away and come back to the solution. If I have a confrontation at work, I don't react immediately. I will take time to think about it.
Beverley

Taking anger in your stride

As Beverley and I walked together, I frequently upped the pace of our physical progress around the park. She was a reasonably quick walker to begin with, and I felt that this was her natural way of needing to channel out anger and stress.

When anger dissipates, the pace can be slowed, allowing the adrenalin that has been pumping to drop a few levels. If necessary, it can be upped again during your walk until you are calmer and feel your anger has been channelled appropriately out of your body. I call this fast/slow approach interval power striding, and I'd like to show you how it's done.

EXERCISE: INTERVAL POWER STRIDING

The exercise is similar to high-intensity interval training which is common in many gyms and workout classes. Researchers from the University of Texas say that high-intensity exercise has a positive effect on a protein called brain-derived neurotrophic factor (BDNF), higher levels of which are linked to improvements in cognitive function, leading to reductions in stress, anxiety and anger levels.

Some preparation is needed before starting this exercise as it involves walking at a fast pace. If you have any medical conditions which might be compromised by walking quickly, please check with your doctor before you begin. Also, it's important to diarise your stress, anxiety and anger levels (from 1 to 10) before you start the exercise and to keep this up. Keeping a log will increase your personal discipline and sense of reward as you see your ongoing progress.

1. Walk at a gentle, comfortable pace for five minutes.
2. Continue walking at a slightly faster pace for another five minutes, or until you can start to feel your lungs inhaling and exhaling oxygen more frequently.
3. Now walk as quickly and intensely as you can for one minute, focusing on channelling out any anger, stress and uncomfortable negative energies your body might be holding on to.
4. Quickly reduce your speed to a gentle, comfortable pace for as long as you need to catch your breath, but not so long that your body starts to cool down.

5. Repeat these steps as many times as you feel able, but no more than five times to begin with.

Once you've done this a few times (either alone or with a friend, family member or colleague) and noticed your stamina increasing, you can tailor the exercise to suit your own requirements.

Now read what Ryan thought about interval power striding:

Striding forward with a sense of purpose was a great way to release the stress and strains I felt during a maelstrom of work stress. At a time when I was weak and vulnerable, increasing the pace of walking definitely helped me to reconnect with my power and channel my aggression. By the end of a walk, I always felt lighter and better for it.

Ryan

It's important to remember that nobody's perfect. Everyone makes mistakes and has regrets. But what matters is that you learn from them and don't wallow in self-pity. You can create as many opportunities for personal change as you need. Learning how to express your feelings more effectively in different situations and reflecting what you could have done better is a work in progress. It requires, time, effort, commitment, practice and, most importantly of all, resilience and perseverance.

CHAPTER 6: DEPRESSION AND DISCONNECTION

*Depression is being colour blind and constantly
told how colourful the world is.*
Atticus Poetry, 'Love Her Wild'

The flipside of anger, and one of the major consequences of our efforts to suppress it, is depression. Of all the mental-health difficulties arising from our stressed, overworked and target-driven twenty-first century society, depression is the one that seems to grab all the headlines, generating more and more statistics proving how this has become an epidemic of global proportions.

A *Times* newspaper investigation in 2018 revealed that in England alone, more than 7 million adults were treated with antidepressants the year previously. This was an increase of almost half a million in three years. According to the World Health Organization, some 300 million people worldwide suffer from depression, and it is one of the leading causes of ill health across the planet. Shockingly, this crisis is worsening for children and young people ranging between the ages of ten and twenty-four years old; figures released by the NHS in 2018 showed that almost 400,000 in England were being treated for mental-health problems.

I don't think it would be an exaggeration to say that everyone has had the experience of depression at some stage in their lives, either within themselves or through someone they know. It is everywhere and appears in many forms, ranging from general low mood and persistent feelings of sadness to more extreme conditions such as bipolar disorder, mania and manic episodes, all of which can lead to self-harm or even suicide. Male suicide, otherwise referred to as the 'silent killer' is one of the single biggest causes of death for men under the age of forty-five in the UK, and is three times higher than female suicide. The most recent Suicidal Statistics Report released by the Samaritans in 2017, showed that in 2015, there were 6,639 suicides in the UK and the Republic of Ireland. Of those, almost 5,000 were male. This highlights the sensitivity in men who may struggle to vocalise their feelings as a result of male pride and the need to be seen as 'strong', or the fear of being vulnerable and seen as 'weak'.

Note: before continuing this chapter, please let me advise that it is vital that feelings of depression, however mild or severe, should be checked out and properly diagnosed by a mental-health professional such as a GP, nurse, counsellor, psychotherapist, psychologist or psychiatrist.

What is depression?

Depression can be defined as low mood, loss of enjoyment in life and reduced energy, lasting for two weeks or more. It can range from mild depression, where your work and social life might be affected but you can still function, to a more severe form, where you can barely get out of bed, never mind think about anything else. Clients of mine who have suffered from symptoms of depression have often commented on their feelings of malaise, despair, constant sadness, lack of direction and hopelessness.

If you took away a wolf's pack, then its environment, plus its ability to hunt, to demonstrate anger or fight back, you would then witness a very different type of animal – one that has been stripped of its identity. Similarly, depression can take away the memory of who a person used to be, placing them in a lifeless tunnel of void, where they question who they've become and how they're going to move forward in their life once again. All in all, depression can leave a person feeling disconnected and disassociated from themselves, their family and friends, and even life itself. Life can feel pretty pointless at times; and in the more severe stages of depression, it can feel as if it's not worth living at all.

If you see a GP, it's highly likely you will be prescribed antidepressants or be referred to a mental-health specialist for a full assessment. Any GP should always suggest a course of counselling alongside antidepressants. Antidepressants are *not* a cure for depression and shouldn't be seen as a long-term solution. They help to alleviate the symptoms, but they don't address or tackle the root causes of the problem. With perseverance, patience and courage these can always be worked through with a mental-health professional. How long it takes is down to the work and action you put in and the severity of the depression. Your GP will be able to assess how long you need to take antidepressants for, which will be reviewed every three months. Whatever you do, don't suddenly stop taking them without consulting a mental-health professional first.

So let's check in with how you are right now. If you're low or depressed, try your best to describe how this feels in your own words, either below or in your Walking Diary:

At the moment I'm feeling low and/or depressed. And this is how it feels:

....
....
....
....

You may not know at this stage what has caused your feelings or how they developed. But if you do have some insight into what's behind your depression or low mood, write below what you believe that may be, for your own personal clarity. This will also be useful and beneficial if you intend to seek further help in the future.

I'm feeling depressed/in a low mood because:

....
....
....
....

Based on years of professional observation, my view of depression is that it arises as a result of the classic 'pressure-cooker' situation, as described on p. 86. We expend a great deal of time and energy repressing anger that exists because of childhood trauma, difficult life transitions or external pressures in our day-to-day lives which cause stress. As we saw in the last chapter, the energy generated by feelings of anger must go somewhere; if it is constantly pushed down, it will either 'blow', leading to an episode of rage, or it will continue simmering, resulting in prolonged periods of depression. Because of genetic predisposition and family history, environmental factors or a general lack of self-esteem and self-care, some people are more prone to depression than others. And if you're one of these, chances are that you have felt too ashamed to open up about how you really feel. Worse still, you may have tried to self-medicate with alcohol or drugs. We have come to know this as 'drowning your sorrows'. Unfortunately, however, in many cases those sorrows never drown – if anything, they come back harder, darker and very quickly learn how to swim.

Victoria is a perfect example. She was diagnosed with clinical depression at the age of fifteen – one hell of a label to give a child of that age. Known as the 'sensitive one' in her family, she was sent for counselling sessions in a clinic, but her alcoholic, chaotic mother insisted on sitting in on the sessions, making Victoria feel traumatised and unable to open up:

> *The therapy sessions at the clinic were*
> *horrendous. I just cried and never talked, so*
> *I was never able to understand my feelings. I*
> *was scarred by this experience. Everyone said*
> *I was depressed, and at seventeen I was given*
> *antidepressants. These didn't seem to work, so*
> *the dose was upped.*
> **Victoria**

As we saw in the Introduction, it was clear from our first few sessions that face-to-face therapy with Victoria in an enclosed space wouldn't work. Her earlier experiences of this had traumatised her to the point where attending this type of therapy actually increased her distress. Walking outside really helped to alleviate her tension, and it wasn't long before Victoria began to open up and share some of her story, particularly related to her party lifestyle. Here, she elaborates on what she said earlier:

I looked into the reasons why I was drinking and partying hard. I would happily go out every night. I would just say 'Yes' to anything. I never thought anything of it; for me it was just going out for a few drinks. But some nights would get really loose and if anyone was having a party, I'd be there. I'd go out all night and give myself no recovery time.

I felt I had to tell everyone that I suffered from depression. I had to tell my work because sometimes I'd just burst into tears for no reason and have to go home. I felt I had to tell every boy I dated because sooner or later it would become obvious. And I was surrounding myself with friends who constantly wanted to go out. It really was a downward spiral.
Victoria

Alcohol – best friend or worst enemy?

Before anything else, my advice to Victoria was to stop drinking immediately. This was not going to be easy. Drinking gave her the confidence she was missing in her day-to-day life; she felt she couldn't 'be herself' without a drink on board. What she didn't realise was that drinking to feel confident and to alleviate her feelings of depression was a short-term solution, and that in the long term it would actually make her feel worse. Drinking alcohol is a very common way of attempting to manage depression, but when we drink, we are putting a depressant into our bodies. And drinking a depressant to manage depression will always end up increasing, not decreasing, such feelings.

Of course, we don't know this when we take our first few

sips. We feel comfortably numb and more upbeat, so we drink more. But this is what actually happens: alcohol encourages the release of dopamine the 'feel-good' neurochemical, along with adrenalin, which is both a natural stimulant and a 'painkiller' – a painkiller that also helps to temporarily alleviate difficult and painful emotions. The depressant part of alcohol relaxes the nervous system and also disrupts the part of the brain called the 'pre-frontal cortex', resulting in lowered inhibitions, inability to accurately assess situations and increased aggression. The problems that can develop when someone is in this state are obvious – and then comes the crash. The 'high' induced by alcohol is quickly replaced with a 'low'; depression and anger return and are exacerbated by the alcohol. We wake up the following day feeling worse than we did before having a drink. Unfortunately, at this stage, many of us will self-medicate again in the worst way possible – by having another drink. And if we repeat this cycle and start drinking regularly, our serotonin levels will decrease rapidly, leaving us with almost permanent low mood.

Victoria was masking a huge amount of low self-esteem but couldn't see this because she was clouding her issues with alcohol and continuing to feel depressed. She made a really big effort to stop drinking, and very quickly she started to realise how alcohol had contributed considerably to her feelings of depression:

I started to make better choices, particularly towards exercise. I exercised every day when I was growing up, because the more clubs I joined, the more time I spent away from home and my mother. I stopped exercise when I was diagnosed with clinical depression – I got into a rut. Then I started again, and in a big way.

There were times during this period when I did go out and drink and would get depressed immediately afterwards. Then I'd think, 'Oh fuck, this is why!' and realise I could reset myself to the person who was exercising and working through this. I realised the importance of having a clear mind; you can't focus when you're hungover.

Victoria

Depression has a very strong element of fear and isolation attached to it. In her state of depression Victoria was certainly more fearful that if she stopped drinking, she would be alienated from her friends and have no one to turn to when she felt down. But rather than keep these feelings to herself, which would have left her feeling more isolated, she decided to be open and honest about her depression. And I greatly admire her courage for making it publicly known to friends, family and work colleagues about how she was feeling during this time. Many others (men in particular) will never admit to feelings of depression. Despite all the talk, there is still a massive stigma and feelings of shame attached to the label. And men's innate pride and desire for people not to see them as 'weak' holds them back from discussing feelings they are uncomfortable with.

Learning to open up

The need to 'hold it together' is a very common excuse for many people who find it hard to vocalise or show their feelings. They will go to extraordinary and damaging lengths to be seen as infallible and as someone who is 'always in control'. But over

99

time, the unrealistic expectations that they place upon themselves will inevitably take their toll on their mental health, and
in many cases this can lead to depression and even suicide. The
shame in potentially being seen as 'unworthy' by others if we
are struggling emotionally or feeling vulnerable, is something
we need to challenge ourselves and others on, taking a risk to
be more open and honest about our feelings.

Trust plays a big part here. You need to trust that you are
brave enough to reach out and ask for help, and trust the
person you're reaching out to, even when your inner critic is
saying, 'I mustn't show weakness. I must go into work. I must
look after X's needs, because if I don't everything will fall apart.'
You worry that people will find you strange for revealing your
vulnerability – but believe me, those who are able to acknowledge their difficulties and ask for help are among the strongest
people on the planet. In my experience, when one person opens
up about their feelings, this gives licence for someone else to
talk about theirs too.

Being brave enough to show your true self in your positive
moments *and* in your darker moments makes you who you are
today – imperfect, different and unique. And guess what? We're
all imperfect and different. So it's better to be honest rather than
to pretend any more. Sometimes you need take a bold step,
demonstrate a less popular stance, maintain your boundaries
and ruffle a few feathers in order to 'reset' yourself, to borrow
an expression from Victoria.

Ryan, whom we met earlier, had been suffering from
depression for a long time when he first came to me. He sought
help from his GP, who suggested he take some time off work.
Sensibly, Ryan agreed, and that time out, along with his
enthusiastic take-up of Walking Therapy enabled him to really
'uncoil', as he put it:

*I became more open, and then things went in a much
more positive direction, and it was all part of that
process of talking things through. And exercise,
getting back to nature, noticing things, being
conscious of breathing – everything that was layered
in at the time. For me, it was a major change and it
made me reflect on my sexuality, so I've accepted
myself. I now have a partner and he and I are getting
married in a couple of months.*

*When I started therapy, I felt unlovable and
Jonathan pointed out that I needed to develop a
loving relationship with myself first. This made a
big difference. Then, later on down the line,
when I met my partner, we fell for each other
and that was it.*
Ryan

If you're depressed, or know someone who is, you will understand how isolating yourself can exacerbate your feelings.
My mother battled with depression (unsurprisingly) alongside
the cancer which finally killed her, and I remember how
powerless I felt to not be able to help her. I also remember
how frustrated and angry I felt at not being able to talk to
her about the complex feelings I could see she was experiencing, and regularly sensed her frustration and anger at not
being able to verbalise her emotions. She was always one for
being seen as strong, even though I could see when she was
clearly struggling.

Depression creates a feeling which is best described as that
of being 'stuck'. Many who have been depressed refer to it as
'wading through treacle'. They know full well that they're

depressed, and that psychological knowledge, plus the physiological effect it has on their bodies, keeps them demotivated, isolated, indoors and locked away both in body and mind. Remaining indoors also means that far less light is received through their retinas, and melatonin (the hormone that regulates the sleep/wake cycle) and serotonin levels drop, leading to a state similar to that of seasonal affective disorder (SAD), which is itself a form of depression.

So what's the answer?

Difficult as it may seem (and I know how hard it can be when you're feeling low and sluggish), one way to counteract depression is to force yourself out the door and get moving. If you were stuck in mud, you wouldn't just stand there and wait for help. You'd try to drag yourself out, even if you lost a shoe in the process. It's the same with depression: by moving forward physically (in terms of walking) you help to unstick yourself psychologically by recognising that there is a 'way forward'. I'd suggest walking each day for a minimum of one hour, but do what you can. And by setting yourself this daily goal, you will start to reclaim a little bit of self-esteem.

Telling a person with depression to 'be positive' is like ordering a storm to be calm. Have hope that the storm will pass, and even though it may not feel like it, you are, in fact, far more powerful than your depression. Anxiety and depression are a part of you, not all of you. It may feel hard to conceptualise right now, but having hope means you will find your way out of this. By stepping outside, you're making the first move towards a better, clearer future.

So now let's see how you might walk towards achieving this. Firstly, you can revisit 'How to Walk' in Chapter 2 (see p. 34), where we walked confidently and with purpose, even if we didn't feel like it. Some call this 'fake it to make it' but I prefer the term 'Pygmalion effect'. This derives from Greek mythology, where a sculptor who had no success with women fell in love with one of his creations. He wished her to become real, and the goddess Aphrodite granted his desire. Put simply, the Pygmalion effect is another term for a 'self-fulfilling prophecy': if you walk confidently – head up, shoulders back – and at a decent pace, you will feel more self-assured and positive. This might not last, but the more you keep doing it, the longer and greater the effects are. Trust me, it works.

Another exercise to try is walking and feeling present. This is a good exercise for combating stress, but it also works well for depression, in which internalised stress acts as a major catalyst. Identifying where in your body you may be experiencing repressed or difficult feelings can help you to explore and understand what other feelings are adding to your current state of unease.

EXERCISE: WALKING AND FEELING PRESENT

1. At the beginning of your walk, I would like you to stand still and take a moment to mindfully scan up and down your body for signs of stress or unease, asking yourself the following questions:

- Where in my body do I currently feel it?
- What type of feeling is it?
- Is it acute, dull or slight?
- Is this the only part of my body that is currently experiencing feelings of stress/unease/low mood?
- What emotions can I link to these feelings or

sensations in my body? (For example, anger, sadness, loss, frustration, overstimulation, exhaustion or shame?)

- How would I rate the level of low mood from 1 to 10 (10 being my lowest mood)?

2. Next, focus on one of the areas you have pinpointed and start walking. For example, let's imagine you've identified it as a kind of dark cloud occupying your brain. As you walk, exhale deeply and visualise expelling the darkness, or dark clouds from inside your head. As you walk, really try to visualise them leaving your body, trailing behind as you continue to walk forward. Don't try to consciously solve any other problems or come to any resolution for the time being; instead, focus on naming any other emotions that may become more apparent as you're walking.

3. Midway through your walk, once again stand still and put a new rating next to the feeling you identified earlier. If it's lower, repeat the process as many times as you need to or until you feel it has lightened. If you have the motivation or time, focus on a different feeling in your mind or body that may have come to light during your walk, and repeat the process.

4. At the end of your walk, slowly bring yourself to a standstill, sit down and be proud of what you've just been able to accomplish while in the presence of natural surroundings. If you can maintain this practice daily, you will be able to recognise your ability to feel more connected and present in all areas of your life.

Let's go back to Matt's Walking Diary to see how he connected with the Walking and Feeling Present exercise. Note how he keeps his observations simple and to the point:

21 Nov

Where I'm walking: by the canal.
For how long? One hour.
Where do I feel my depression? In the middle of my stomach.
What kind of a feeling is it? Kind of a sick feeling. Making me feel too ill to do anything.
Is it acute or dull? Dull – but there almost all the time.
Any other areas of depression? Sometimes in the head. A dull ache. Feel sluggish. Can't be bothered to do much. Reminds me of the weather this time of year.
What emotions do I feel? Sadness, lethargy, loneliness, feeling hopeless.
Rate the level of depression: About 7. Not a good day, but not one of my worst.

As usual, Matt wrote down his thoughts at the end of the walk:

How do I feel now I've finished? Definitely better. Depression level improved to about 4. Still feel tired but noticed a few things that sparked my imagination. I saw a half-sunken bicycle in the water. Something about it reminded me of myself – half in, half out of life! It made me laugh a bit – it's not easy to laugh at yourself when you're depressed but I did, and I felt better for it.

Matt's observation about the bike half out of the water is interesting and leads us to the final exercise in this chapter. As we know, it's always useful to check in with how you feel both at the beginning and end of a walk and where possible, to record your feelings. By doing so, you will begin to build a picture of your recovery and see how it's progressing. So at the end of Walking and Feeling Present, have a think about anything you've seen along the way which has captured your attention. Draw this in your Walking Diary and write down how it might represent how you're feeling right now.

When you take your next walk, have a look around to see something that gives you *hope* for a brighter future. Matt told me that on one of his city walks, he spotted three children offering a group of workmen a bottled drink they said they'd bought with their spending money. It was a very hot day and they'd seen the men working hard under the midday sun. 'Something about it, and the workmen's grateful reactions to this group of city kids really touched me,' he said. 'It reminded me of a time when I was young and would do spontaneous stuff like that. I feel if I tapped into that kind of innocent energy again somehow, my depression would just clear off.'

Whether it's kids showing random acts of kindness, objects that you come across (such as the feather Tianna found – see p. 56) or the young boy who saved my life through the gift of empathy (see p. 14), when you walk outdoors, these miracles can happen if you're open to them, and you can be deeply affected by them. They can be life-changing. You may find yourself suddenly reconnecting with feelings of warmth, love and happiness you'd long forgotten, reminding you of times in your life when you were carefree and allowed yourself to live in the present, not worrying about past or future events.

When I designed the Walking and Feeling Present exercise, observing how nature transformed over the seasons became, for me, the most therapeutic part of the process. I understood that everything has a life and a death, and that things would come to an end, but life would begin again. In a way, I had a spiritual 'death' and rebirth during my depression, which I now understand had to happen. Very often, if you break down you also break through – and that's exactly what happened to me. My depression wasn't pleasant at all, and neither is yours, but have hope that you will emerge from it a stronger, wiser person. And don't forget to stick your head out of doors – walking with a bit of purpose will generate the energy you need to make a good recovery, at your own pace and in your own time.

CHAPTER 7: CHANGING TIMES, CHANGING LIVES

Progress is impossible without change, and those who cannot change their minds cannot change anything.
George Bernard Shaw, Irish playwright, critic and political activist (1856–1950)

The only certain thing about life – aside from death – is that it is uncertain. Although we all try, none of us can really control our futures. Even if we retreated to the most remote place on earth in the hope that we would experience a simple, unchanging existence, we would still be subject to variations in the weather, availability of food and shelter and incursions by other people.

For good or for bad, change is inevitable. Yet so many of us are blindsided or laid low when we go through difficult transitions. Mostly, we amble through life assuming we're on the 'right path', expecting things to go to plan – and when they don't we become angry, stressed or depressed because we feel 'out of control'. When facing major adversity, allowing ourselves to face up to difficult feelings and ask for help is a good thing; after all, the onset of a serious illness, the loss of a career or a relationship are certainly not to be taken lightly, and we all need extra support and comfort during these times, however proud we may feel.

Yet even when our world is shaken to its core, it is how we choose to interpret these 'life transitions' that is important and this can have a significant bearing on how we manage them in the present and the future. We can either embrace the need to change or fear it. We can see it as inconvenient or invaluable. It is my view that we need to fully embrace change and to adapt by taking action, rather than procrastinating. Our intuition, along with our desire to thrive and survive, will guide us through this process if we choose to engage and listen to the 'wiser' part of our psyches. The more we develop a relationship with our gut instincts, and trust in them, the richer this relationship will become in our ongoing adaption through life. As Charles Darwin said: 'It is not the strongest of the species that survives but the most adaptable.'

Accepting that life transitions can be challenging is the first step in coming to terms with the concept of change itself. It is often our fear of endings and fear of the unknown that prevents us from embracing it. We spend far too much time in our comfort zones, not daring to look at the 'wildness', inside or out, for fear that it might somehow harm us. But how do we know that for sure, unless we step out of that zone and towards our fears?

The wolf is, by any standards of the animal kingdom, an excellent parent. Cubs are cared for devotedly and any which die prematurely are often buried by mourning members of the pack. Indeed, the whole pack takes on the rearing of its young and a vital part of this is allowing them space to explore their world and learn to adapt and be resilient to it. The cubs are, quite literally, pushed out to fend for themselves. They must develop quick responses to fast-changing situations – or die.

Most of us pay little heed to our 'wildness'. Unlike the wolf cubs', our very existence isn't usually so acutely threatened and therefore the need to adapt becomes less vital. Because of this, many of us can become far too content remaining within our comfort zones. Which is why, when we are faced with sudden adversity, we may feel fearful and low in confidence that we are able to cope with and survive these difficult life challenges.

Remaining within our comfort zones will only increase our fear of investigating our full potential, and full wildness. That is why life has its own way of pushing us out at times to encourage us to face and survive our fears, just like the wolf mother does for her cub.

When change comes, or is forced upon us, it is amazing what we can achieve if we open ourselves to adaptation. In the wild too, animals draw on their instinct to adapt very quickly to fast-moving situations. Those who experienced the Christmas 2004 tsunami in South East Asia vividly recall seeing animals and birds fleeing the shoreline for higher ground, long before any human realised the gravity of the situation. On a different tangent, I went to the 2012 Paralympics in London and was totally inspired by seeing athletes with disabilities perform to such an incredible standard. These people faced challenges in their lives, but they chose to adapt to what for many of them was a new situation in the most positive way possible. While most of us may never face a dramatic change such as losing a limb, the truth is that we are changing all the time. That's why I hate the term 'mid-life crisis'. We are always adapting and changing, whether we like it or not, and it can be hard seeing these transitions in 'real time'.

Some changes are more profound than others, and how we interpret and negotiate them determines how well we adapt. Are you currently going through a change in life? If so, describe it in the space opposite, and how it is making you feel:

My change in life is:

....

....

....

....

And it's making me feel:

....

....

....

....

Remember that every period of change feels 'new' – almost like you're seeing it through the eyes of a child for the very first time. At first, you might be fearful, but if you constantly rise to the challenge, that fear you initially experience will eventually be replaced by confidence in a situation that has now undergone a change of some kind – even if that change is unknown to you at the time and is out of your awareness.

When I had my own 'crash', following my period of addiction to drink and drugs, the change in my life that scared me the most was that I felt completely on my own. Most of this I was responsible for, by pushing away everyone that I loved and sabotaging anything good in my life, but at the time, destruction was the only thing I felt I had full autonomy over in my life. Yes, I had lost people I loved, including my mother and brother, but that was no excuse for my behaviour and numerous unloving actions towards myself and others. I knew deep down that I needed to change, but instead I clung to chaos as a necessary distraction and deflection from the truth. And the truth was, I was terrified. Terrified that I would look into myself and see the darkness that represented my loneliness and the isolation of not knowing who I was any more.

Looking back, I felt I had something of a death wish, driven by my fear of admitting that I didn't know what to do and that I needed help. My bullshit and denial had finally hit a wall, and I was left not knowing how to exist living a life that would no longer involve excessive drink or drug-taking. In the end, I was feeling so psychologically, emotionally and physically depleted that I was forced to put down my pride and surrender to the truth that I couldn't carry on. Something had to give: the situation had changed, and as such, I would need to embrace change, and not keep running away from it.

As I mentioned previously, when I finally got clean, I discovered that nature would unconditionally support and nurture me through this period of upheaval. It anchored me. When I walked in Richmond Park, through the trees, I knew that even if I lost every material thing, I would still thrive in this place. Sometimes when you have nothing, you suddenly realise that, in fact, you have everything.

Within our lifetimes we are all going to be forced to confront our deepest fears, whether we like it or not, and will have to find the resilience to survive them. In the woods, we are surrounded by both light and dark or shade. And just as the woods embrace this mixture in order to thrive, so must we. For life itself is made up of light and dark experiences.

For me, being in the woods connects me completely to my primal self. My intuition is immediately heightened and although I know I'm alone, I also know that I feel protected and nurtured. While delivering Walking Therapy sessions over the course of the year, I love to watch and feel the seasons change, and to notice how they are also a metaphor for the spiritual death and rebirth of each individual that walks beside me. The woods have often represented 'the unknown' – and what we don't know, we can't control. So perhaps we should simply let go of our rational selves, trust our intuition and walk deeper into the forest through times of transition.

Jerry's world was one of high pressure, constant meetings and decisions made in an almost permanent state of stress. His realisation of this brought him to a momentous conclusion:

The rise of email and tech and the rise of coffee all go hand in hand. If you are able to be relaxed, and if you're de-caffeinated, you might go to a typical business meeting and think that your colleagues are actually insane. I've seen this hundreds of times. The people in charge seemed sociopathic; they were hyperactive, talking over each other, not listening at all. People don't realise the extent to which they are being controlled by software designers. There are legions of people in Silicon Valley whose job it is to make people feel harried and hurried and needy via social media. And people don't understand they are the targets of these people who are trying to fuck with their brains.

I knew I had to get out of that kind of environment. It's a war. I feel clever taking myself out of this game and I feel smart for doing it. I feel I have a new and improved mind.
Jerry

It is fear that drives us into stress mode when the opportunity for change comes, or indeed is forced upon us in some way. When dramatic change occurs, we often believe that the safe worlds we have built for ourselves will fall apart. Maybe they will, but the hope is that they can be replaced by something more nurturing if we choose to seek it. Beverley's realisation that she could embrace a change in her working life was a revelation to her:

> *I think I now have much more self-belief. I have many skills that can be transferred into a lot of places and I can leave. I can go. I couldn't have seen this before Walking Therapy. I was a one-dimensional being before this. Burnout is one-dimensional – you can't think of anything except work. Now I'm not worried about working in Starbucks if I have to. I don't have to stay at this, I can just leave. I'm in a position where I've saved money – if I couldn't work for six months, that would be OK.*
> **Beverley**

The authentic (and inauthentic) self

Everybody has an authentic self, but sometimes life goes off course and you find yourself in a state of inauthentic self. For example, you might have been bullied at school or in the workplace, but instead of fighting back you bullied someone else. It's a way of adapting to what you think you need to do to emotionally survive. I've had clients who've worked in all different types of jobs that involve many stresses and pressures, and there always seems to be a point in their careers when they wished to return to a moment that had meaning for them – in other words, searching for a path that would lead them back to their authentic selves. More often than not, their response to Walking Therapy has been amazing – immediately, they look and feel like they've 'come home' because they're finally back in the environment that at one point in their lives nurtured them and looked upon them without judgement. What I've learned through this is that, for one reason or another, nature seems to be a common denominator in every-one's lives, where most people come back to seek some kind of sanctuary through the process of transition.

You may not be aware when you've drifted away from your authentic self and ultimately how you would like to be living, but you instinctively feel it. Your mind and body react with either discomfort, stress or anxiety, knowing full well that you're living an inauthentic life. And you can often feel destabilised and unsettled during these times of transition. It's like tectonic plates beginning to shift before an earthquake. You just feel it – you know something is amiss. The emotional shift is happening, and events are moving forward. You can either choose to move with them, and experience everything that change and transition brings, or you can continue with your feeling of being 'stuck'. At times, it feels like you're not moving through this transition quickly enough, but usually that's down to a degree of impatience that society thrusts upon you. It's called 'conditioning'. Subconsciously, you always seem to look at the person beside you and say, 'Why are they so sorted? They look confident and happy.' But what you will never see is the softer side of their soul. You'd rather look at the harder shell and compare your strength against it. Protecting your more vulnerable self is like a comfortable coat you've worn for years. That coat comes in many different shapes and sizes and that is what makes you 'imperfectly unique'. And you need to embrace that vulnerable self with both arms, especially through times of adversity.

I've been abandoned more times than I care to remember. Loyalty seems to be very thin at times, and this is why you need to always remain steadfast and stand up for the more sensitive parts of your soul. If someone else chooses to judge you through any transitions you may face in your life, this says something about them, not you. It's the integrity in what you believe deep within yourself that will always be your guide. So please don't ever forget that. Yes, it's lonely, but you will realise in time and with patience that your authentic self needs time to come to fruition. All you can do is trust the process and have faith that at some point it will come right.

Because I have faced a lot of change and adversity throughout my life, writing this chapter and talking about transitions has been difficult, as it has forced me to recall and revisit changes and challenges I have had to face and overcome. But it has also reminded me of my resilience and what we can all endure when faced with challenging moments in our lives. I think I will always fear change, even though I have learned to trust in it. I used to be controlling, out of the fear of losing control, but I now know the point at which I need to surrender and let go.

I have always feared letting go of something or someone that I have loved or felt connected to. But sometimes you have to address the reality that what you love and think is helping you is, in fact, hurting you. This was certainly my mindset when I decided to give up alcohol and drugs. You may ask, how do I know if the important life decisions that I make are the right ones during each transition? The truth is that you don't, but you need to have faith in yourself and trust your intuitive feelings. It is in these moments that I've needed to be steadfast, restating to myself repeatedly, 'I will not abandon myself'. And by this, I mean: 'I will trust in the decision that I make.'

I can honestly say that with every life transition I've gone through I've stood by what I 'believed' and remained true to what my 'gut feeling' was telling me at the time. It's like any external relationship. Trust takes time. It takes a long time to build but can very quickly be broken. And that is why, whenever the world is screaming at you to be someone you're not, you need to take a leap of faith in who you ultimately feel you were destined to become. And this is where you need to trust in and do right by yourself and take the next best step. If you can't trust yourself, how can you possibly trust others?

The seasons and life transitions

It's interesting to see how change seems to occur at certain times of the year; winter seems to be a time for 'introspection', whereas the period after Christmas and the coming of spring is often the catalyst for new beginnings on a personal level.

Sometimes I say to clients during our process over the course of the year, 'Think back to this time last year, and look how far you've come', and they can hardly believe the transition they've been through in just twelve months. Significant dates, too, often prompt major shifts; birthdays and anniversaries are particularly fertile occasions for personal change.

When we go through change, we find we're in a process of constant renegotiation with ourselves and our circumstances. And we must accept that we too have changed over the years. Our priorities have shifted, our goals aren't what they were, we feel differently about life. And such inner changes can be hard to accept, along with external shifts such as growing older, experiencing children moving away from home, etc.

So with all this being said, to fully understand the nature of transition and how it makes us feel, let's take a walk aligned to change, by exploring paths that we previously might have ignored or rejected. An area of woodland is the best setting for this, as there will be twists and turns in and around unknown routes. Alternatively, if you live in the city, you may choose to explore a different route on your way to work or at the weekend, in and around your local area. During moments in my life where I've been 'playing it safe', I would always find myself choosing the same walking path, not veering away from it, avoiding any risk and not showing any kind of spontaneity. And at other times in my life, where I have been known as a risk taker, my walking routes have been quite the opposite and I've found myself exploring more freely like I used to as a child. This is what we call the 'free child' – free from the rules and laws that often constrain us in later years through the process of conditioning.

EXERCISE: WALKING INTUITIVELY

In this exercise, I want you to make a choice between taking the most efficient or the most exciting path: the one that will either take you most efficiently to your destination, or the one that will take you on more of a journey. I want you to ask yourself:

- Why have I chosen this particular path?
- How does it represent how I'm currently living my life?

For instance, if you are someone who struggles to manage your spare time or work life effectively, are you going to choose the shortest, most efficient path? Perhaps you are currently lacking in creativity and would therefore prefer to play it safe as that doesn't require any strategic thinking? Or are you craving change in your life, possibly an adventure that would encourage you to break away from an old routine that has left you feeling trapped within your daily life?

Keeping this in mind, I would like you next to solely focus on your walking steps. Look at the ground and watch your feet try to negotiate the most exciting route to take. I did this recently and found myself sidestepping paving stones, up and down various slopes, connecting with a far more carefree side of myself and with nature. This is a mindfulness exercise that requires intuition, spontaneity and creative thinking. It will also help you to let go and face your fear of the unknown, as you're never completely sure where you're going to end up.

When change is in the air, we are very often unsure of where it will lead us and, as I've said, it is that uncertainty which drives fear. However, we can choose how we interpret this uncertainty. It needn't be the way of fear; instead, we can look at change as an opportunity to discover something new about ourselves or develop something we knew we were capable of, but never had the opportunity to try out.

EXERCISE: WALKING WITH VISION

The next exercise is one of creative visualisation that employs the Pygmalion effect previously discussed (see p. 103). It will help you to redesign how you see yourself now in your mind's eye and how you see yourself in the future. Remember: if you see yourself in a negative light, you create a self-fulfilling prophecy whereby the predictions you make about your destiny often come true, influencing all your present thought processes, decisions and actions.

The good news is you can also create a 'positive' self-fulfilling prophecy by choosing to see yourself in a more positive, aspirational light. Let's see how this process works:

1. At the beginning of your walk, try to visualise how you currently see yourself, how you look aesthetically and how you go about your daily life. The more detail you can create in your mind's eye the better, so try not to rush this process.
2. Throughout your walk, think about the stages and actions you need to take to get to where you want to be. To begin this process, try to ascertain which parts of your life leave you with a feeling of contentment and which leave you with one of frustration, fear or disappointment.
3. Focusing on the parts that tend to have a negative impact on your psyche, I want you to visualise how you'd like to change these aspects of yourself. Try to formulate more positive images of yourself to replace older, negative ones.
4. Having followed all the previous steps, now visualise how you see yourself in your future, and where you would like to be in five years' time.
5. At the end of your walk, I would like you to quickly compare how you saw yourself at the beginning to how you see yourself now.
6. When you get home, write down and collate all the information from your walk, and devise a clear and strategic plan of what you now need to change and the steps you need to take to get to where you want to be in five years' time.

I worked on the Walking with Vision exercise extensively with Matt. He and I walked in woods close to his home. At first, he found the trees heavy and oppressive, yet quite naturally he slowed down and commented that whatever he said to me seemed to be 'soundproofed' by the woods. I understood this to mean that he was beginning to feel protected in that environment, and that he found it a safer place to open up than he'd previously thought. Here is an extract from his Walking Diary that day, which includes this exercise:

16 Feb

Where we walked: Seven-Acre wood, close to my house.

For how long? One hour.

How I see myself before I set off: Lonely, generally just 'down', getting by. I don't make much effort to look good, but neither am I a total scruff. I could brush up well if I wanted to – but I don't much want to.

During the walk: I talked about the fear of losing my family and being on my own. I visualised myself as a kind of hermit. Am I happy with that? Some aspects of 'hiding away' appeal, but I like company too. I can see myself wanting to 'heal' alone, though I'm not sure how healthy that would be.

Where would I like to be? If my partner and I can't work it out and get back together, then I hope we can get on OK for the sake of our son. For myself, I'd like to be confident that I'd be a good single dad. I'd like to live without tension and arguments. I don't want to be on my own for ever, but I don't want to fall into a relationship that won't work out just because I feel lonely. When I was young, I used to paint and draw a lot – I'd really like to find out if I'm still any good and see what happens.

How I feel at the end of the walk: I feel there are more possibilities for me than I thought. I know I've got to deal with this break-up, and that I'll feel pretty low at times. But many people break up and it's not the end of the world. I'm beginning to see that change isn't all bad.

How could I achieve this? I'm going to stop all the arguing with my partner and accept that while life can be difficult, problems don't last. I'm going to think very carefully about where I want to live and what I really want from life. And I'm going to sign up for a painting class. I think I'll take a lot of comfort from getting back into my art.

You can use this exercise to remodel or change any aspect of your life. Using powerful imagery in your mind's eye will unequivocally change how you feel emotionally, and the more you repeat the exercise, the more clarity you will gain as a result.

Negotiating with and navigating transition is not easy. So many things may be happening at the same time that you wonder what you've done to deserve them all. Coming out of addiction into what I now consider a spiritual rebirth, I certainly wondered what was going on. And believe me, I did my very best to resist it. At that stage, I thought the universe was against me. Whereas if I'd listened to my intuition and had the courage to accept that change is a fact of life and not something to fight against, perhaps my transition would've been less fraught.

The universe reminds you of the things you can't control, and that sometimes you just have to sit back and trust that you will come through the other end of the transition. Everything happens for a reason. I've seen this so often with clients, as well as in my own personal experience, and it's given me immense strength as a therapist. My clients' courage and determination inspire me. And it's comforting to know that quite often, the most you need to do to facilitate effective change is simply to surrender to it. And you can do this. Let go. Take a chance. See what happens.

CHAPTER 8: GRIEF AND LOSS

*It is impossible to go on as you were before, so you
must go on as you never have.*
Cheryl Strayed, *Tiny Beautiful Things*

In any change or life transition there is always a grieving process, and it is during this that we are ultimately forced to confront an 'ending' of some kind. As one chapter ends, another begins. Yet at the moment we turn the page, we may suddenly feel reluctant to do so, because none of us finds change easy, and especially the process of 'letting go'.

Grief can include anything we consider a loss, and the depth of loss is always proportionate to the significance and depth of connection or the attachments we make on our journey.

Then there is grief for those we have lost to death. If we lose a job, we can regroup, dust ourselves off and apply for another one; if a relationship breaks down, we can learn from the experience and meet someone new. There are even times when we may grieve for experiences we never had in our lives. But when we lose a person to death, not only is that relationship severed for ever, we also lose a part of ourselves that cannot be replaced.

Grief, shock and shame

The same set of stages are present in all aspects of grief. At first there is shock and denial. Next comes a period of anger – that feeling of betrayal and injustice ('Why did this happen to me?'/'Why did you leave me?'/'Why did you have to die?') – followed by depression, as the reality of the loss sets in. Finally, there is acceptance – where life goes on and we must do our very best to go along with it, at times begrudgingly.

However, not everyone experiences grief in such a linear way. Some may experience anger or depression for longer than others or find themselves unable to surrender to their sorrow, bottling it away until it comes out at an unexpected moment. As we anxiously make comparisons to validate whether we're grieving 'properly', this may lead some of us to experience shame and to believe there is something innately wrong with us, which can be both disempowering and destabilising at a time we need validation, strength and support the most.

There is no 'right' or 'wrong' way to grieve. Some cultures grieve closely as a community for an intense period, creating an outpouring of grief; others are more focused on being alone and finding a place of solace and solidarity. Instinctively and intuitively, what we ultimately desire is to be rid of our grief and to find 'release' from the uncomfortable feelings we carry. But this can often be at odds with our other impulse to 'not let go' for fear of losing control of powerful emotions such as anger, loss, injustice or sadness. It's sometimes hard not to fear facing up to powerful emotions as they come to surface, and it is completely normal to want to repress some difficult feelings as they arise. We fear 'letting go' of these emotions because to do so would be to admit what we have lost. So repressing them is another way of remaining in denial and avoiding the finality of death.

I would describe this as 'keeping the wolf from the door'. Here, the wolf represents primal energy: instinctive emotions we have learned to repress to protect ourselves from experiencing shock, disbelief, upset, feelings of vulnerability, exposure, embarrassment, coming to terms with a difficult reality, or at other times to protect loved ones from worrying about us and to distance them from powerful feelings with which we don't wish to burden them. Do we also fear we may somehow embarrass ourselves publicly? We are often told that it is 'OK to cry, but not to be angry' or it is 'OK to be angry, but not to cry'. Whatever the expectations are of how we're 'meant' to feel, how many of us in the moment feel the courage to vocalise our feelings in front of others?

I have experienced three episodes of bereavement-related grief in my life and every one of them left me feeling different within myself, and how I saw the world during that time. However, going through the process of grief has helped me come to terms with the fact that dying (and loss) is a natural part of life. What is important about each bereavement is the 'message' left behind by the person who has just died. Did they live their life to the full? Did they experience all that they wanted to experience? Did they want more time to address regrets they had in their life? Did they reflect on those friends and family members that they lost touch with? Or did they die with the same spirit as they had chosen to live their life? When I worked as a therapist in a hospice, it was very common to hear people expressing their wish to have experienced more in life, to have had fewer regrets and to have kept closer contact with family, friends and loved ones.

You could ask yourself similar questions about other types of loss too. Below are a few suggestions that you might like to consider:

- Did what you lose somehow contribute towards the person you are today?
- What memories do you recall best about whom or what you recently lost?
- What has this loss taught you so far about yourself, or how you would like to live your life?
- What message do you think has been left for you?
- Is the loss you've experienced currently stopping you from moving forward, and if so, why?
- Intuitively, what type of support do you feel that you need to help you move forward in your life once again?

If it helps, write these questions in your Walking Diary as a reminder to think about them when you're next out.

Grieving and reconnecting

I was only seventeen when my mother died and, naturally, I went into shock. In that moment, I realised the power of the bond between a mother and her child which had now been taken away from me. My last words to her before she died were, 'I love you and I'm very proud of you'. She was very weak, but responded to me, 'The same'. After that, I emotionally disconnected from myself and my family members and, as I've said, drank hard to numb the pain. I felt betrayed by her leaving me at such a young age, mainly because her death felt so unjust and untimely. Alcohol exacerbated my anger and turned me into a human wrecking ball. Even though it helped me to escape a painful reality that I wasn't willing or ready to face, it also turned me into a different person who went out of his way to annihilate any healthy relationship or spiritual connection in his life. When I sobered up, all I could do was observe the destruction and misery I had created for all. Alcohol had become one of the most unhealthy, toxic relationships in my life, but one that I simply didn't care to question at the time.

When my eldest brother died, I inevitably drank even harder to prevent myself from experiencing any more feelings of loss and sadness (I will talk about this again in the next chapter). After all, there was only so much loss or heartache I could take. In retrospect, I only wish I had found a better way of dealing with my feelings during this time. But I was young, and simply didn't have the emotional tools to cope. Although, to be honest, it's not even a question of age, as one's life experience, knowledge and wisdom can all fall by the wayside if the pain, loss or heartbreak are great enough at any point.

When I was ready to change, being out in the open helped me to understand that painful loss wasn't the universe summoning up its darkest forces against me; rather, it was just part of life. We win, we lose. We live, we die. It's sad, but it's part of the life cycle of every living organism.

Walking helped me to get in touch with my memories by getting rid of all the distractions that can occur when someone dies, and at times it felt as if those I'd lost were walking alongside me in my thoughts. It reminded me of walks I'd had with them and all that we talked about. During my walks, I remember thanking them for all they had brought into my life, and even though I was sad I would never see them again, I knew that I would always treasure and remember the messages they left behind.

During the process of grief, it is vitally important that you don't avoid the 'ending'. By this I mean saying 'goodbye', which can be done in a way that is meaningful to you individually.

Writing a letter to a loved one who has already died or creating a ritual of some kind that defines the relationship between yourself and the person you have lost are healing ways to create or establish that the person you loved is no longer with you. This is also applicable to any other life event where you're experiencing an 'ending' that you're struggling to come to terms with.

A client, Francis, had recently lost Ann, a great friend of thirty years, to cancer. Before Ann died, she asked Francis if he would write and deliver the eulogy at her funeral 'because', she told him, 'you'll probably be the only one who will hold it together on the day'. He laughed because – as always – she'd got him spot on. He was never very good at displaying the 'right' emotions when required. He knew, and so did she, that any outpouring might (and only might) come much later, once the proverbial dust had settled.

Francis and I walked across the shore near his home and along a beautiful, yet dangerously slippery, coastal path. It was January, and the sea and sky blended into the same shade of lead-grey. I asked him where he felt he was in the grieving process.

'Everyone else has done it,' Francis replied, 'but I seem to be the only one who hasn't experienced the whole breaking-down thing. I can't find it in me. Not being able to – somehow being cut off or blocked from it – is driving me mad. I feel like I ought to and should do. But I can't. It doesn't come naturally, and it doesn't feel right.'

Francis's difficulty was that he felt guilty and ashamed for not grieving 'properly'. Compounded by this was the fact he didn't attend Ann's funeral. 'The day she died was the same day I left for a family holiday,' he explained. 'I was away for three weeks and I knew I'd miss her funeral. I'd promised her that I'd read out the eulogy, but it wasn't to be. I feel I broke a promise to her.'

I noticed Francis found it hard even to say her name, and I asked him why that was. 'Speaking about "Ann" in connection with her death makes it all too real,' he said. 'I can't seem to accept that she's gone. I'm not so much sad as angry. Plenty of people die before their time, I know that. But her? It doesn't seem fair.'

When Francis met Ann, they had both just left home for the first time. Ann was an easy-going and carefree person who brought her lightness to Francis's life.

'She made me laugh,' he said. 'Simple as that. We had a great private humour between us which was never lost, even at the very end of her life. It was a love affair without the affair bit. So just pure love.'

We walked at pace up a long incline leading to the top of the cliff. I explained to Francis that the inner voice telling him he 'ought to' feel distraught about his friend's death seemed non-empathic to the depth of their relationship, putting unnecessary pressure upon his grieving process. I also pointed out that placing heavy expectation upon himself by using the words 'ought to' or comparing his experience of grief and loss with another person's could create shame – a feeling designed to belittle, disempower and lower his sense of worth by its constant ridiculing that he is 'not doing it right'.

'I'm not sure it's "shame",' he said. 'I don't feel ashamed about anything; it's more about feeling bad that I can't seem to grieve properly.'

'OK, let's look at it another way,' I said. 'Supposing your inner voice was coming from a real person – a parent perhaps?

And they were saying, "You haven't cried about this – why not? Is there something wrong with you? You really should feel bad about that." How would you feel?'

Francis paused. The waves pounding against the far side of the bay appeared to echo his conflicting thoughts.

'I'd feel terrible,' he said finally. 'Like I'm being told off – really punished. I guess I would feel ashamed. And angry too.'

'Why angry?'

'Because if this is a parent talking to me, you'd expect them to have more sympathy or understanding. I've lost a great friend. Surely that's enough?'

'OK,' I said, 'so if this isn't a real person talking, but your inner voice, and you know what it's telling you is wrong, why are you paying attention to it?'

'I don't know,' Francis replied. 'I can't answer that. It's just there.'

I asked Francis whether feelings of shame creep into any other parts of his life. He told me that he very often pushes himself too hard at work, seeking perfection in everything he does.

'It's made me successful at what I do,' he added, 'but it doesn't always make me happy. It pushes me on, which is fine, but sometimes to the detriment of other things.'

Gently, I guided Francis towards the idea that he was perhaps internalising feelings of anger which have now developed into a critical inner voice that admonishes and shames him. I explained that Ann's appearance in his late teens represented a 'broadening' of his outlook on life. Intuitively, he understood that moving out of darkness and towards the light would be beneficial – in this instance, that 'light' was Ann, who radiated it in abundance.

'I get all that,' he said. 'But it still doesn't explain why I can't cry for her.'

I told him that not everyone responds in the same standard way. 'Be patient,' I said. 'The tears will come when they're meant to come, if they come at all.'

I explained to Francis that patience is key. Rushing to find a 'solution' means, more often than not, pushing away deeper feelings. In nature, time is the healer. Observing the feelings of loss, and noticing their presence, is often far more reparative than trying to find a quick fix to externalise them. Feelings of loss, anger and injustice are never comfortable emotions to experience or sit with. Yet they are testament to the closeness of the relationships we have with those we have lost.

As we walked down the slope towards the small seaside town, closed up for the season bar a few cafés and pubs seeking trade from winter walkers like ourselves, I asked Francis what message might Ann have left behind for him? We paused by the sea wall while Francis considered his answer.

'Physically, at the end she was too weak to say goodbye,' he replied. 'But if she'd had the capability, she'd have said, 'Enjoy life. Embrace it, and others too. Be kind. Be generous. And don't always be so virtuous, either!'

'And how can you take these ideas forward into your own life?' I asked him.

He grinned. 'I've already started,' he said. 'When I'm in a situation where I'm taking myself too seriously, I think, What would SHE say about this? And then I can't be serious for much longer.'

In this way Francis is learning to hear a different dialogue

– the one which spoke to him when his friend was alive, pushing away his critical, admonishing inner voice. By listening to *her* voice, he can now respect, embrace and pay tribute to the gifts she left behind for him. He is discovering that his sadness is useful, after all.

Several months passed before Francis contacted me again. He wanted to let me know how he was getting on. This is an extract from his letter:

> *The dam didn't 'burst' for ages. Then, about a month ago, I went to see a theatre production of* A Monster Calls. *I was OK up until the final scene, and then the tears just poured out. But as the lights went up, I could see I was far from the only one crying. At that moment, I knew I wasn't alone. We'd all experienced something life-changing and heartbreaking.*
>
> **Francis**

Living with loss

When you lose someone or something you love, it can seem unimaginable to conceptualise life without them. People in grief often describe how sadness hits them when they least expect it, like a stab to the heart. The same goes for feelings of deep loss and anger, as you realise that something or someone is missing from your life. Out of nowhere you may feel stunned, shocked or disconnected from those around you, or feel isolated and alone.

EXERCISE: WHERE DO WE SEE OUR LOSS?

On your next walk, take a moment to recognise where you sense or see that feeling of loss or 'void'. For example, if you've gone through a divorce, is it a happy couple walking down the street that makes you feel sad or empty? Or if you've lost a parent, friend or loved one, do you feel more drawn to notice a family or social group laughing in a café? If you've lost a job, do you feel envy or jealousy towards those you see going to work in the morning? If you feel sad that you're getting older, are you noticing more the vibrant youngsters running ahead of you?

Below, or in your Walking Diary, identify when and where you've experienced any of these, and how they felt:

Where and when did I feel my sense of loss?

....
....

How did I experience this?

....
....
....
....

How did it make me feel?

....
....
....
....

Once you've ascertained where you see your loss, next time you experience this on a walk try to attach positive memories to it, instead of focusing negatively on what you no longer have. Ask what this moment reminds you of, the times you shared and what you took from these experiences. At some point during our lives, we will all lose something or someone close to us that holds great significance, but we don't have to lose the happy memories attached to them. We have the power to make this choice.

Anyone who's lost someone close will have experienced the phenomenon of 'hearing' that person's voice, or even 'seeing' them in a place they used to frequent. I'm not talking about anything ghostly – this is more about association with the deceased person and the triggers which bring him or her back into real time. Sometimes this can be unsettling. On the other hand, it can give comfort and a sense of familiarity to the person affected.

EXERCISE: WALKING WITH LOSS

When you next take a walk, in whatever environment you choose, try to visualise the person you've lost in that setting. Do you see them striding through the city, ambling along a beach or trekking through woods? How do they look? What are they saying to you?

Once you've done this, take time to reflect upon their spirit, and what you feel is the 'message' that they're trying to convey to you. Identifying the message they leave behind can help you make contact with the wiser,

> more philosophical part of yourself, and give you a more
> confident, clearer life perspective and outlook. It may
> also provide comfort to you.

I asked Francis the questions from the Walking with Loss exercise about Ann. 'Oh, I can see her in the sea,' he replied
immediately. 'She's there, having a paddle, encouraging us all to
take off our shoes and socks and join her. And bring down
another glass of gin and tonic! What's she trying to say? I think
it would be, "Enjoy life while it lasts!"'

Creating an ending through rituals or symbolism

When you feel ready, during your next walk, try to consider
how you could mark the ending of an era or significant chapter
in your life by creating a ritual that's pertinent and personal
to you.

When you suffer a loss of any kind, it is vital, as I've said, to
confront the ending. This will help provide you with a sense of
closure and allow you to say goodbye. A funeral is itself a ritual,
but it may not feel personal or private enough for you to say
goodbye and mark the uniqueness of the relationship with whom
or with what you have lost. This is where creating a more person-
alised ritual really helps.

Some might write a letter that helps to outline and define
their emotions, and once they've written it either burn it, wrap
it around a stone and throw it into a lake, place it in a bottle
and send it out to sea or bury it in a place that is significant to
them. There are no rules and you can be as creative as you want.
Some might like to create a time capsule of memories by placing
photos or objects that hold significance into a box and hiding

it in a favourite spot out in nature; others may just go to the pub on their own or to a favourite restaurant and make a toast to mark the end of a special relationship.

Creating a ritual also marks a commitment to move forward in your life. You can still visit your memories from time to time, and experience your feelings connected to your loss, as long as you're still going out of your way to live life to the full. Making a commitment such as this helps to remind you that you still have the power and confidence to get things done during any time of adversity.

This is how Francis responded to the idea of a ritual to mark Ann's passing:

> *I knew there was to be a charity walk organised in Ann's name, so I decided to join part of the route. It would be challenging, but nothing compared to what she went through while she was ill. It was the best thing I ever did. I met up with old friends, we laughed and talked – a lot about Ann, but also about our own lives too – and we toasted her when we reached the top of a long climb. I'd tied an animal-print scarf to the top of my walking stick (she loved animal print) and we used that as a kind of flag. Then we got hopelessly lost and we laughed some more: we really felt her mischievous, accident-prone spirit at that point. At the end of the walk, we all felt we'd achieved something quite special. She will never be forgotten, and neither will the bond between her friends.*
> **Francis**

Walking with your grief in the ways described here is healing and can truly help you feel that you're moving forward in your life. Being outside in the fresh air can provide a neutral environment in which to think and process feelings, and the act of movement and 'striding out' can help to reconnect you with a feeling of empowerment. By walking slowly, you feel calmer and soothed by the sounds of nature; and increasing the pace during your walk can make you feel physically stronger than you do emotionally during times of adversity.

When you grieve, you can often get trapped in a 'tunnel vision' of stress. Going outdoors can encourage you to feel less stressed and experience a wider perspective. If you feel alone in the world, naming the trees, a lake, a hill or an area that has sentimental significance for you can help you reconnect with nature and the more spiritual part of yourself. As ever, nature is the universal parent and reconnecting with it can help provide you with the feeling that someone is always looking over or walking beside you.

CHAPTER 9: NEVER ENOUGH – THE GRIP OF ADDICTION

*Addiction is when you can't get enough of
what you don't want any more.*
Deepak Chopra, Indian-born American author and
alternative medicine advocate

I hesitated for a long time before finally deciding to write a chapter about addiction. We've heard quite a bit so far about self-medicating with alcohol for work-related stress, anxiety and depression, but at what point does a glass or two each night to unwind tip over into something more problematic?

Having been an addict, I understand what lies beneath it and how unbelievably difficult it can be to beat it. At one time or another, most of us experience the kind of stresses and strains described in this book, but how many of us will say they've been addicted to something? Or perhaps more pertinently, how many of us will *admit* to being an addict?

Describing someone's behaviour as 'addictive' very often results in arms being thrown up in horror. Why? Because most of us consider addiction to be a term that only applies to someone else. A typical response might go something like, 'I'm *not* an addict. All right, I like a glass of wine or two every night – OK, maybe half a bottle or so – but I can handle it.

I've got a very stressful job and it just calms me down, that's all. It's not as if I'm a debauched alcoholic, hiding my drink from everyone or waving a plastic bottle of full-strength cider about.'

No, you're not the same as this wreck-head of an individual you're currently comparing yourself to – or are you? Perhaps you're both relying on something to get you through life's challenges, and while you can hold down a job and function at a less chaotic level than our cider-drinker, is there really *that* much different between your needs and theirs? Aren't you both hiding behind the bottle?

The same goes for drugs. Believe me, there isn't a huge gap between a few 'cheeky lines' at the weekend and finding yourself in a crack den in the middle of the afternoon. I should know – I've been at both ends of the spectrum, and one can very quickly lead to the other when you least expect it. And yet, those people who use drugs recreationally, so to speak, would be the first to dismiss any notion of drug addiction. 'Oh, come on,' they'll say to me, 'what's the problem? Everybody's at it these days.'

The rise in recreational drinking and drug-taking

Alcohol is more available and affordable now than it's ever been: 29.2 million adults in Britain had an alcoholic drink in 2017, and almost 1 in 10 adults (4.9 million people) say they drink at least five days a week.[6] This same survey points out that people in professional or managerial jobs are most likely to have had a drink in the past week. Yep, that will be all the people trying to manage stress, anxiety and depression, then . . .

The statistics concerning drugs also make for sober reading (if you'll pardon the phrase). The NHS reports that in 2016/17, around 1 in 12 (8.5 per cent) adults aged 16 to 59 in England

and Wales had taken an illicit drug in the last year. Hospital admissions for drug-related problems have gone up by 40 per cent in a decade and deaths related to drug misuse are at their highest level since comparable records began in 1993.

Addiction is everywhere. Which is why I decided, ultimately, to include this chapter. Because the truth is, you don't have to fit the stereotypes to be addicted to something, whether it's booze, drugs, tobacco, gambling, sex, work, TV, food, money-making . . . Obviously, there are healthy and unhealthy, as well as high- and low-level addictions, but when all is said and done, if you're relying on something to dull the pain of everyday living or to escape reality, it's fair to say that you're demonstrating signs of addictive behaviour. In the words of actor and comedian Russell Brand, 'Drugs and alcohol are not my problem; reality is my problem, drugs and alcohol are my solution.'

As I've described, we tend to choose not to see our addictive behaviour because we're constantly comparing ourselves to others. We might wonder whether we've a problem, but when we think about one of our colleagues, friends or family members, who always seems to be 'on the lash' (as well as being 'hammered' 'bladdered' 'battered' 'slaughtered', 'trashed') we comfort ourselves with the fact that we're not like them. If you look at these terminologies, aggression is clearly associated with them. Addictive behaviours seem to help us find a sense of release from the internal frustrations, stress and aggression that at times we may find hard to process or vocalise during our day-to-day lives. In other words, we're looking for the right thing, but in the wrong place. Fear and the inability to manage thoughts and emotions play a major part for all who struggle with addiction issues, and it is usually a feeling of shame that prohibits one from admitting this to another.

The 'hierarchy of shame'

Someone who looks down on another person for what they see as their failures creates what I call a 'hierarchy of shame'. And this is applicable at work, home or socially. We place ourselves at the top and someone else at the bottom, as is often the case within society, especially around status. We tend to do this to make ourselves feel 'more than' rather than 'less than'. For example, we may think, OK, maybe I drink or take drugs, but I don't do them as often as so and so, or get into as big a mess. Or, I have never or would never do things in the way someone else has done. But if we're really honest with ourselves, I am sure that at some point we have all done exactly what we are disdainful of in others. And the reason we sometimes find it hard to accept or admit some of the less proud moments in our lives is because we feel 'shame' about them.

The hierarchy of shame is an effective way of not looking at or avoiding our own self-destructive or imperfect behaviours. To my mind, it's incredible how people with more 'socially acceptable' addiction issues will judge those with addiction issues deemed 'less than' by society, especially those who suffer from alcohol and drug addiction, and put these people way below themselves in the addiction stakes.

I meet a lot of people who are in denial about their own addiction. They're aware they have problems; if it's drink, they know that alcohol is a depressant and that using it to medicate for stress, anxiety and depression is, in the long term, completely counterproductive. Yet they refuse to admit they have a problem, and certainly don't want to give it up. 'Me, an alcoholic?' they say, shocked. 'That's impossible. I only drink two glasses of wine a night.' But it's not impossible. One person can have exactly the same amount of alcohol as another and react in a completely different way. If you're waking up feeling terrible, you go to work hungover, your moods are generally black and negative and all you look forward to is the next drink to make the pain magically disappear, then it doesn't matter whether you're drinking a bottle of the finest claret or two litres of cheap, potent cider – you've got a problem and you need to deal with it right now.

The addictive personality

Is there such a thing as an 'addictive personality'? Some refer to those who tend to be more extreme in their addictive behaviours as having a mental disease, or a disease of the mind, while others use the term addictive personality to describe those – usually in their peer group – who engage in regular recreational drinking and drug-taking or other addictive habits such as gaming, gambling and sex. But at the end of the day, however you label it, it inevitably leads to the same downward spiral. And what I see most commonly is emotionally challenging life events that very quickly turn a harmless habit into a harmful nightmare. It's even possible for someone to be addicted to their own adrenalin, drama or extreme behaviours, which can create a self-perpetuating cycle of anxiety and distress.

In my experience, conditioning in the early years gives a child the propensity towards addiction and dependency in later life. When I was a young boy, I noticed that most of the adults close to me drank alcohol – to be sociable, yes, but also as a way of dealing with difficulties. At the age of six, I was presented with a little wine glass and was allowed a drop at the table during dinner. No one thought this unusual or harmful back then, as many didn't have the knowledge we have today. If truth be told, a lot of people are still in the dark about the severe consequences that drinking alcohol can have at any level, and from any age.

I don't blame my parents for allowing me drink at such a young age. They didn't feel it was wrong either; as I've mentioned alcohol wasn't then seen as a serious drug. Yet I was a shy, sensitive boy who realised that a drop or two of alcohol soon put paid to that and gave me confidence in spades. Add to this the stress caused by my failure to perform academically, the bullying and later, my mother's illness and early death, and you have an almost perfect recipe for more destructive, addictive behaviours, exacerbated by an increasing desire to avoid difficult feelings. Whether there is an element of 'personality' in there is hard to say – certainly, alcohol released me from my innate shyness, but it also opened the door to a more dangerous world. A world in which the darker aspects of my wolf appeared. Once drunk or high, I would prowl, hunting for the next party or next fix. At night, my wolf felt completely alive, but after alcohol and drugs, it turned into menacing behaviour towards myself and others.

The thrill of risk, danger and chaos was something I wanted more and more of. It also gave me a 'sense of purpose'. When the world I knew was falling apart, and I was losing all sense of power, alcohol and drugs were things I had control over. Under the influence, I always thought it was my primal instincts that kept me alive and away from badly harming myself or others. But in fact, it was the opposite. If you sedate a wolf and pump it full of drugs, what do you have? An animal stripped of its primal instincts and attributes, one that is a total liability to itself and others.

I've found in my practice that the more sensitive you are as a person, the greater your sensitivity to alcohol and how it leaves you feeling over a period of time. As I've said, two people in very similar circumstances can have the same amount to drink and react in wholly different ways, depending on their degree of sensitivity. For me, it was extremely detrimental to my self-esteem and how I viewed myself. I think that no matter what my life circumstances might have been growing up, I probably would have ended up addicted to alcohol and drugs. It is something I have to be aware of and manage every day, so as not to fall back into it. In my case, there's no respite.

With that in mind, let me tell you about my brother.

My brother's story

Richard was loving, sensitive, funny, sarcastic, charming and highly intelligent. He was religious – a devout Catholic – and a music lover like my father. Richard was also gay, and because of his religious devotion he struggled with the shame of this. And he drank; drank to push away the shame, and to allow himself to come to terms with his sexuality under the influence of alcohol. He was always challenging other people's boundaries, mainly because I think he lost sight of his own over time, as can happen with ongoing and excessive drinking. It certainly did in my case.

His drinking, like my own, became chaotic. And there were many occasions where this was witnessed by others. I remember vividly when my mother died, he told me he'd never get over it, as they'd always been extremely close. When he eventually came out as gay, his sexuality was accepted with open arms by our family, after which he made great efforts to curb his drinking and get himself together. He hadn't quite put down the firm boundary against his alcohol dependency, but there were signs that he was finally becoming the person he was always meant to be.

And then a few short years later, and on the day before the anniversary of my mother's death, he went out for a drink or two. Someone sold him a quantity of methadone at a bar. He wasn't a heroin addict, so he had no reason to buy it. I will never know the exact circumstances, but I can guess what happened. Richard wouldn't have known what methadone was, or how it should be used, i.e. sparingly. Perhaps through bravado, and wanting to push his limits, he would've taken the mixture sold to him in one go.

Methadone killed my brother, but if he hadn't been a drinker, he wouldn't have swallowed it. Alcohol is what we call a 'gateway' drug to other experimental drug-taking, as it lowers your inhibitions and therefore increases the risk of self-harm and even death. He wasn't at all streetwise. He was a lovely, sensitive, innocent guy with a problem that indirectly killed him. What a waste.

In full-blown addiction myself at the time of my brother's death, instead of wising up and turning my back on the whole chaotic mess that alcohol had left my family in, my reaction was to embrace it (and drugs) wholeheartedly. I would tell people that I didn't want to live beyond twenty-eight. I didn't know it then, but I was actively trying to commit slow suicide. I thought I was in control. I was far from it, clearly. In retrospect, I now understand that by doing this I was subconsciously re-enacting Richard's death to gain a deeper closeness and understanding of what he'd been going through at the time, and regain a sense of control over something I'd felt powerless to prevent.

Addiction can be defined as no longer having control over a habit to the point where it could cause you harm. And to recognise this doesn't necessarily require that you wake up in a pool of your own vomit, or with a stranger in your bed and no memory of how he/she got there. Your addictive behaviour may be the cause of constant arguments at home. It may adversely affect your bank balance or your health (or both). It may be the source of missed promotions, lost opportunities and failure to reach your potential in life. It could well be affecting the lives of your children and immediate family.

There's such a stigma with addiction, it is almost impossible for family to give you the empathy you need when you're going through it. You're abusing and betraying yourself, of course, but you're inevitably doing the same to those around you. People who live with or are otherwise close to a person going through addiction feel as much stress, trauma and the general sense of everything being out of control as the person they're supporting. This is commonly known as post-traumatic stress disorder (PTSD). When I was going through my own addiction and I went out to drink or take drugs, no one knew if I'd end up alive or dead. For anyone trying to live with such uncertainty, the stress is unimaginable.

I recognise I have an addiction – what next?

The answer is simple. STOP. Stop putting yourself in the way of harm by turning your back on the thing that is controlling your life. Not next week, next month or next year – stop *now* and seek help immediately.

I understand that whatever you're addicted to makes you feel confident, happy and alive when you're doing it (and makes you long for it when you're not), but you must remember that all you're doing is *masking your true feelings*. You feel depressed, you have a drink, you feel better, then you are even more depressed the next day. You buy something online, it arrives, it makes you happy for five minutes, then you're looking again for something new. And while you're doing this, you're not tackling the root causes of your compulsion to drink, take drugs, spend, gamble, whatever. So first, you need to stop. Right now. It's what I tell all my clients and I'm very black and white about it. There is no hope of getting to the bottom of what's eating you up unless you remove the mask first. You say you 'aren't ready to do this yet'. I say, 'Then come back to me when you are. Because at the moment I can't help you.'

I hope this doesn't sound harsh. What I learned is that the only way to tackle addiction is head-on, facing up to the consequences of your actions.

When I was in the throes of addiction, it was like standing behind a large plate of toughened glass, watching my life disintegrate. I witnessed the hurt I did to myself and others, and at the time it seemed like there was nothing I could do about it. I felt utterly powerless. But when I made a clear decision to stop using alcohol and drugs, that gave me the power and courage to repair these areas of my life over time. I was helped (after rehab) by a support network of a few close friends, family members, community support groups and continued counselling sessions. Joining any community – whether a local club of some kind, art classes or college, for example – helps greatly, as it satisfies the need for a sense of belonging which is essential in ongoing recovery.

Stopping whatever you're addicted to or dependent upon tends to follow a cycle of change (a model put forward by Prochaska and Di Clemente) which runs in the order of pre-contemplation, contemplation, preparation, action and maintenance. Pre-contemplation is where you're in denial and convince yourself and others that you don't have a problem. Contemplation is where you are slowly coming out of denial and starting to realise that you might actually have a problem. Preparing what you need to do to support the changes you wish to make and taking action around these decisions is next. And then, maintaining your recovery from an addiction is key. If you don't, and you relapse, more often than not you return to a state of denial, convincing yourself once again that 'I don't have a problem'. And the cycle repeats itself. The length of each stage can vary, of course, but my advice would be not to linger when getting to the 'action' stage. The quicker you do it, the less time you'll have to procrastinate.

It was very clear that I had to stop drinking and going out all the time. I just needed a clear mind, but you can't focus on anything when you're hungover. It was a chaotic time. Once the drink stops, you can create a framework of stability. You can create order in your house for yourself. For me, getting back into exercise was huge. I'd stopped exercising, partly due to feeling depressed. When I finally stopped drinking, I'd book a gym class at 6.30am, which meant I couldn't get drunk the night before. Driving was a good boundary too when I was going out. It really helped to have that excuse. Since I've stopped drinking, I've noticed that the mindsets of people I know have changed too. Now, it's much more acceptable not to drink and get drunk.
Victoria

Victoria had many underlying difficulties with her mother, but when she was drinking, she couldn't address these properly. Without the alcohol, these issues were still real and painful, but Victoria could allow herself to be angry *and* speak coherently about it. It was then that she began to set clear boundaries for herself and others.

Support groups and communities

My own journey included many meetings at Alcoholics Anonymous. It might not be for everyone, but all I can say is that it worked for me. Rehab centres are fine, but they're not always great on support and maintenance (aftercare) once you're out. AA and equivalent organisations are free communities of like-minded people from all walks of life who are there to help and support you. I attended many, many meetings and just enjoyed the feeling of turning up, putting the kettle on and making the tea, arranging the chairs and being part of something that made me and others feel valued, respected and supported. There is an emphasis on a 'higher power', which many people interpret to be God (hence many consider AA a cult, which couldn't be further from the truth). For me, however, this higher power lay in nature and walking outside.

Goal-setting

Creating a personal goal and setting yourself an achievable length of time to abstain from addictive behaviours, will create a window of opportunity to see what your life is like without an unhealthy addiction. When you drink alcohol and take drugs especially this creates 'ego-distortion'. Ego-distortion is exactly what it says – it distorts reality and ruins personal clarity. Once you have achieved a good amount of time abstaining, reflect and note down what your life has been like since. Has it benefited your relationships with others? Has it increased productivity at work? Do you feel more connected to life in a way you never thought possible? These are good questions to ask yourself once you've achieved your goal. 'Go Sober for October' or other events such as these that raise money for charities may also give you encouragement and support to stop for a period of time with others if you're finding it difficult to do it on your own.

Walking with addiction

Being an addict is like walking into a tunnel that becomes narrower with each step. The experience of normal, everyday life lessens as the addict's focus intensifies on that which makes him/her feel better. They lose any connection with everything around them; nothing else matters other than the next drink/drug/bet/etc. And, as we've seen in previous chapters, losing a connection to the environment – the places we walk in, the air we breathe, the elements we see and feel – means losing a vital connection to our inner selves. When we lose our way through addiction, we also lose the physical, psychological and spiritual paths that nurture and sustain us through bad times and good.

When I was hungover and shattered from the comedown of drink and drugs, having the energy to maintain a regular walking schedule was the last thing on my mind and quite simply unsustainable. I lost my ability to manage virtually every aspect of my life, even the simplest daily tasks.

During this period, my therapist told me that it was vital I changed my patterns of behaviour. No longer could I walk to the pubs I used to frequent, no more could I visit the people who supported my life in addiction. I had to find new routes, new paths. As it happened, walking on Wimbledon Common or in Richmond Park were new experiences for me, even though I'd walked them many times before. The difference was that I now saw these environments in a new light. Consciously, I became 'present', seeing everything around me with fresh eyes, and that, combined with the nostalgia I had for the days when our family walked here, before our troubles began, re-established my connection to nature and helped me to heal.

As with recovery from depression, returning from addiction can make you feel isolated, lonely and insular. You feel the loss of the thing you were addicted to acutely; a similar feeling to the end of an intense, thrilling love affair. You feel that things can never be the same again, that there is a huge void in your life that cannot be filled. But that isn't true. If you swap all the focus and intensity you had for the thing you were addicted to with getting outside and walking, you will rapidly see results.

When they put their minds to it, ex-addicts can achieve anything they want because they have the innate drive and determination to do it. As I mentioned before, I believe we are all born with an addictive nature, seeking pleasure and reward in some shape or form. Therefore, addiction doesn't have to be solely negative; it can, in fact, be extremely positive when honed and focused in the right direction. There are, after all, healthy and unhealthy addictions. Victoria swapped booze and partying for exercise and has never felt better. Hers is a story that I've heard repeated time and again – the person who uses their addictive nature to positive effect and achieves remarkable things. If you do this, you're looking for the *right* thing in the *right* place.

Any of the walking exercises described so far are applicable for walking with addiction. You can power-walk or you can amble; you can walk with vision or intuitively. If you've successfully shifted your focus from your addiction, you now have the perfect opportunity to maintain your recovery by throwing yourself into a walking routine that will change your patterns of behaviour and spiritually reconnect you to nature, and to yourself.

There are two particular exercises, however, that are especially good for addiction. They are Walking with Consequences and Walking to the Very Top.

EXERCISE: WALKING WITH CONSEQUENCES

This exercise came out of my own experiences in rehab. I didn't go to some fancy treatment centre set in acres of beautiful parkland. It was gritty and down to earth, and I was convinced that I was in the wrong place when I was told I had to clean the toilets as part of my therapeutic duties. People like me didn't clean toilets, did they? I was quickly brought down to earth by a member of staff, who said, 'Take a look around – all the best decisions you've made to beat your addiction have brought you here'. He was right. That statement had a profound effect upon me, because I simply couldn't sidestep it. My methodology for getting clean thus far hadn't worked. So I needed to stop talking, admit to myself 'I don't know how to get clean' and start listening to the experts and those who had succeeded in becoming drug/alcohol free.

Before then, I'd paid little heed to the consequences of my actions because I was solely focused on getting out of my head. Later, I was asked to write down such consequences. I did, and there it was in black and white

– everything I'd tried to push away or ignore completely. These consequences were now mine to deal with.

So next time you walk, do the following:

1. Use ten minutes of your time to consider the consequences of your addiction.
2. Don't punish yourself – you've done enough of that already. Just make a mental list of everything that went on, good and bad.
3. When you get home, write down these consequences.
4. Keep this list and look at it next time you walk. How do you feel about those consequences now? Is there anything further you can do to make amends? Are there ways of turning any of the negative ones into positives?

This exercise was truly illuminating. It gave me a greater sense of awareness and perspective about my addictive behaviours and allowed me to take full accountability and responsibility for my actions.

And the next exercise is great for those people like Victoria, who are determined to pull something good out of a difficult situation and enjoy a challenge.

EXERCISE: WALKING TO THE VERY TOP

When you're recovering from addictive behaviour, there will be times when you feel tempted to go back to the 'dark side', so to speak, because it's familiar. Or you'll feel stuck in your present situation, not feeling the 'high' that you did when you were addicted. During such moments, you might tend to reinforce a negative internal dialogue, saying, 'I can't do this, I just can't' rather than, 'I can, and I'm going to!' With perseverance, and by placing yourself in a positive environment where you feel supported and inspired, you really can get through difficult periods. It is vital that you create a positive support system within yourself, with an inner dialogue that is strong enough to always challenge your own past negative belief system.

The definition of perseverance is 'persistence in doing something despite difficulty or delay in achieving success'. Therefore, on your next walk, this is what I want you to do:

1. Choose a walk that really tests your physical ability, as this will also test your endurance and ability to push yourself forwards through physical and mental adversity. When you start getting physically tired, this often also tends to increase any negative dialogue you have with yourself, giving you the opportunity to counter it by positive thinking and creating a positive inner script.
2. Before you start your walk, I want you to open your hands and gently place them on your face.
3. Next, start gently rubbing off any negativity your body may be holding on to, as you would if you were washing or showering yourself. Then 'brush off' any residual negative energy from your arms, body, legs and any part where you feel it sticking to your body. Once you've finished, scrunch all the residual negative energy into your hands and throw it away, making the action of throwing as you do so. You are now ready to begin your walk.

4. No matter how challenging your walk is, give it 100 per cent. If you experience a moment where your mind starts to create negative thoughts, compose yourself, redesign that negative script into a more positive one and then recommence your walk.

5. Repeat this process as many times as you need to.

6. When you reach your goal, try your best to allow yourself to be proud of what you've achieved, and allow yourself a moment of happiness by saying, 'Well done' and meaning it. Sometimes, it's good to bring a drink, some food or something that you feel would be rewarding at the end of such a long and challenging walk.

I stopped drinking completely. I don't drink at all now. It was a gift to my friends and family; it's not important to me and I have a happy life without it. I still walk mindfully and spend a lot of time in the park, both in London and New York. You have to be mindful when you've had a crash and created chaos and shame. What you need to know is that you're just a human being having a tough time. To become mindful and always working on yourself and improving yourself is very important. Now I listen to myself and look for the warning signs.
Elliot

When I put my head on my pillow before I go to sleep, I'm grateful for the day I've had and feel good about myself. Every morning that I wake up clean, I wake up with a clear conscience that I haven't hurt myself or anyone else. When I have an appointment, I'm there on time. When someone smiles at me and acknowledges my presence, I smile back and acknowledge their presence also. If someone needs help, I can be available for them. I feel connected to life in a way that is at times beautifully inexplicable. A life without addiction increases happiness, productivity, enjoyment and connection. In short, you live a rich, full and wonderful life without it. And I wouldn't trade that feeling in for anything.

CHAPTER 10: CONNECTING THE SELF, CONNECTING THE SOUL

*To walk the spiritual path is to continually
step out into the unknown.*
Wallace Huey, author of *Unfold Your Wings and
Watch Life Take Off*

Way back in Chapter 1, I introduced three core components of
Walking Therapy that need to work in harmony in order to
bring about maximum benefits for mind and body. These are:

- the psychological
- the physiological
- the spiritual.

By examining how Walking Therapy can bring about significant benefits for you we have effectively covered the
psychological and physiological components of the triangle.
Now it's the turn of the spiritual – arguably the most complex
and challenging of the trio.

Let me state, unequivocally, that I believe in and trust the
spiritual aspect of Walking Therapy. As I said in Chapter 1,
my view is that natural environments can help increase feelings of inner peace and calm, which heighten our connection

to life around us. Of course, no scientist has ever proved that we – and all living things – have a 'soul', but we need only listen to a piece of favourite music, read a much-loved poem or watch a spectacular sunset to understand what it is to feel 'moved' in a way that gets to the very core of human experience. Walking has the same effect on me; something about being out in nature warms my soul and provides me with a knowing and loving energy. My sensations and emotions are heightened with a sense of 'belonging' and I feel part of this world once again. It comes back to the idea of the universal parent – that aspect of nature which holds you in its arms and keeps you safe.

I guess that image offers a clue as to why the examination of the spiritual aspect is often challenging. Simply, some people find it hard to engage with. They understand and accept the science behind oxytocin, cortisol and adrenalin, for example, but perhaps consider the whole idea of the universal parent and its soul-warming energy a bit New Age and somehow incomprehensible.

I understand that. Everyone is different. Some people readily accept spirituality into their lives, while others reject it for a variety of reasons, not least because they've had a bad experience with organised religion or are avowed atheists. In these pages, it isn't my job to convince the sceptic that they must wholeheartedly embrace the spiritual dimension of Walking Therapy. What I would say, however, is that ignoring it or pushing it aside means rejecting an important element in this process – the establishment of an inner connection with the healing properties of nature.

So with that in mind, let's explore an alternative term for spirituality, which is 'connectedness'. Personally speaking, I feel connected to nature when I'm walking in the rain, not caring that I'm getting wet, or when I'm feeling the wind on my face. And I feel connected to others when I'm sitting outside a coffee shop, people-watching in freezing cold weather, drinking a hot chocolate. You might feel this sense of connection when you witness a special moment in nature – glimpsing a deer, perhaps, or a rare bird of prey – or when you meet someone on your walk and share the experience of being in the landscape together, feeling warmed by their smile and demeanour. In therapeutic terms, we call these 'spirit-to-spirit' moments, but for me, the word 'connectedness' feels more digestible.

Please keep the following in mind: that when you feel stressed, you are less present and therefore less connected to different aspects of your life. Walking among nature will help you to vastly reduce your stress levels, enhancing your ability to be 'present' and increasing your sense of connectedness.

Beverley was one of my clients who felt uncomfortable with the 'spiritual' label. In fact, her nickname for me was 'The Hippy', which became a running joke between her and her partner. So we looked at ways of making the spirit-to-spirit concept digestible for her, and she was happy with the idea of connectedness. From that moment, she began to see and feel the benefits that exploring such connections with nature can bring, and within weeks she was noticeably calmer and far more able to talk about her feelings than she had been at the outset of our time together:

> One of the first things I started to do at
> weekends was go to the common and have a
> walk. This gave me time to process thoughts
> and feelings, and I discovered a place
> where I could safely think.
> **Beverley**

In addition to finding connectedness while walking on the common, Beverley rediscovered an interest in art which she had previously put aside because she'd felt she had no time to invest in it:

I've always done lots of crafty stuff and I like to keep my hands busy. I don't really call myself an artist, but I thought about it and enrolled for evening classes in art. I signed up for an oil-painting course, which was so much fun. The creative stuff is the whole spiritual thing for me. That's my spirituality: tapping into my creative side.

Beverley

Katrina was so mired in work stress that although she lived very close to a large green space in London, she'd never actually been there. We made an appointment to meet in the park. At first, Katrina appeared to be depressed and closed off, until a dog playfully crossed her path and she brightened immediately as she bent down to stroke it. In that moment, her demeanour was completely changed, and I reflected back to her the sudden shift in her persona. This was because she'd made a connection to a living thing, which unlocked another dimension of herself. There was a whole different energy around her after that.

Beverley, Katrina and all the clients I've ever walked with benefited from an exchange of spirit or connectedness – call it what you will – that invigorated them, giving them vitality and space to open up and share their difficulties. We've all had this experience; rare indeed is the person who can say they've never been touched by a beautiful view, or by meeting another person with whom they feel they've made an interesting connection.

When this happens, we are suddenly 'in the moment' – we feel a burst of life energy and quite often experience a kind of clarity that isn't there when we're dwelling on past or future events.

With this in mind, let's do a quick exercise in what I call 'Active Listening'.

EXERCISE: ACTIVE LISTENING

When you're on your next walk, either take time to admire a moment in nature (an interesting view, an animal, a bird, a sunrise/sunset) or have a short conversation with someone you meet en route. After you've experienced the moment, do the following:

1. Consider how this exchange has affected you in terms of sensation. Was it warm/acute/cold/indifferent?
2. If it is a strong sensation (either positive or negative), where do you feel it in your body?
3. Walk on for another ten minutes or so, then check in with how you feel. Are you still feeling the sensation that arose from the connection you made? If so, write down in your Walking Diary at the end of your walk how it feels for you now, while it's still fresh in your mind. Did you gain something from it? If so, note that down too.

The object of the exercise is to recognise such moments of connectedness and understand how they affect you. Feeling something, even if it's a negative sensation, is better than feeling nothing at all. To feel connected is to feel elemental and alive, and by making such connections we deepen our sense of being alive through the experiences we have.

My spiritual shift

An example of connectedness from my own life stems from my family's religious beliefs. We were strongly Christian, with my father particularly devoted to his Roman Catholic faith. He was Director of Music at the Brompton Oratory, and I was a choirboy, attending practice and Mass three times a week. As I became older, I questioned the existence of God – my world was expanding, and the walls of the church were confining it. Eventually, I stopped attending and made my own way in life. As a teenager, I strongly felt the need to formulate my own beliefs that didn't feel constricted by any culture, sect or creed.

When my father died a few years ago, something shifted in my spiritual self. My father, mother and brother were now all dead, and I felt that elements of them within me had also passed away. I once again felt sad, angry and disconnected from life. Although I utilised the power of walking in nature to heal a painful wound, something else needed to happen to re-establish my connectedness. One day, I walked into the Brompton Oratory and sat there quietly for a while, thinking about my father. This simple act not only re-ignited the spiritual connection with my father, who loved and had spent so much time in this church, but also reminded me of his love for music that united us as a family and provided us with many happy memories growing up. In many ways, it was my parents' parting gift to us all. Even now, when I walk into any church, I can feel this connection and enjoy thinking about him and the times we spent together. There, I am able to quietly reflect upon the numerous opportunities and gifts he gave me in life, which I feel grateful for and will never forget.

Radiators, Drains and Extinguishers

The spirit-to-spirit connection we feel when we meet someone with whom we immediately bond and who makes us feel good about ourselves is almost magical in its strength. These people are confident in their journey through life (even though they're likely to have troubles of their own; who doesn't?) and because they're generally happy within themselves, they can be happy for others. Such people are known in therapy terms as Radiators. Their energy and zest for life radiate outwards, drawing others towards their warmth and vitality. These are people you want in your life, as opposed to Drains. We've all met a Drain – they are the people whose energy is heavy and life-sapping. They internalise a lot of aggression and enjoy being the centre of any drama, playing both persecutor and victim. Extinguishers are the kind of people who like pouring cold water on your happiness. If you've had a good day, they're always the first to tell you how bad theirs has been.

I don't want to examine these archetypes in depth, but I mention them so that you are aware that they exist and under-stand that the latter two will cause you stress to the point that you will lose spiritual connection. When this happens, especially on a regular basis, you just can't be present because others are sapping your spiritual resources. Walking, of course, helps to replenish them, but in the long term, it is better to consider your relationships with Extinguishers and Drains and see how you might modify them so that your boundaries remain firmly in place.

It's often the case that Extinguishers and Drains don't quite realise the effect they have on others. In fact, most of us are usually unaware of how we're perceived in terms of what we 'give out', consciously or subconsciously. We're sending out signals all the time, via verbal and non-verbal communication, but the only mirror we can hold up to these signals lies within the perceptions of other people. If you're feeling brave, you could try this exercise in which you ask someone close to you how they see you spiritually:

EXERCISE: GAINING SPIRITUAL INSIGHT

This is a simple exercise, but not one to be undertaken lightly. However, completing it might give you quite an insight into what you're putting out for the benefit – or otherwise – of other people. The insights you draw from what you hear may be helpful in terms of modifying your perception of self and reflecting on those aspects that may need to change, spiritually speaking.

1. Ask someone close to you, and whom you trust, to consider how your spirit would be seen if you were to die tomorrow. How would you be remembered through their eyes?
2. When you've got the results, note down in your Walking Diary how this interpretation has made you feel.
3. Note down how you might modify your behaviour as a result.

Matt tried the Gaining Spiritual Insight exercise, asking his sister to be the 'witness' to the effect he has upon others. He told her to be honest, and she was. This is what he wrote in his Walking Diary:

This was a scary exercise to do. I knew my sister would be kind, but also truthful. This is what she told me: 'Matt, you have an incisive and very kind intelligence. While you don't suffer cruelty at all, you do revel in the unusual or bizarre and try to find a funny slant on many things. You are by nature freedom-loving and yet also struggle with freedom, despite being able to fiercely fight for what you believe in. At times you have had to deal with cyclical depression and part of that is knowing what you are capable of and not being able to achieve it. People open up to you and trust your judgement.

Matt told me he found this very helpful. 'I know that I struggle with depression,' he said, 'but sometimes I'm at a loss to know why. My sister pointed out something about this that I just hadn't considered. Now I see how deep frustration brings on low mood, which I feel I can tackle at the root. It's good to know that people trust me and see that I'm a fighter for what I believe in. When you're depressed, you often think that people don't notice you at all.'

Matt's depression has, at times, made him spiritually distant and he has felt unable to connect. He also feels it may have cost him his relationship. Yet, even in despair, there have been lighter moments, and, in a way, his sister's comments have provided the reassurance he has needed for a long time. In life, there are moments when we all need an arm around our shoulder and for someone to say, 'It'll be OK'. Sometimes, it needn't be any more complicated than that.

The spiritual shift Matt has experienced might be small, but it is significant. He has connected with his depression – with what we might describe as the 'shadow side' of himself – and by walking alongside it feels he understands it more. The clarity he has received as a result will, he hopes, lead him to the place in life where he feels he 'belongs'. We've all experienced this – the moment we sense that 'This feels right. Where I am just now feels warm, calm and safe.' When you next sense this, take a moment to appreciate that sensation and, as with the first exercise in this chapter, note down the details in your Walking Diary.

Our 'shadow selves'

When I referred to Matt's shadow side above, I touched on the idea of other aspects of ourselves and how we might explore them. We're all aware that we're affected by things our rational brains can't always understand or explain and yet we feel these things deeply. We know we have different sides to our personalities, and by accessing these we can gain more insight into ourselves. These shadow sides aren't always comfortable dimensions – indeed, quite often the shadow side reveals truths about us that can be challenging and unsettling. Yet if we ignore, deny or push away the shadow self, we lose aspects of our personality which, if managed properly, can be very revealing and exceptionally useful in our day-to-day lives. For example, I know I have a wilder, darker part to my personality which relishes the night time and revels in the exploration of the unknown. My responsibilities in life mean that I can't wander wildly outdoors each evening, but I can explore this side of myself via a metaphor – that of the 'shadow animal'. My shadow animal is, of course, the wolf.

When I was younger, I used to have a recurring dream that I was a wolf. At the time, I chose not to give it a second thought. It wasn't until I was older that I suddenly realised that perhaps the wolf represented my subconscious archetype, shadow side or shadow animal. When I thought about this further,

I understood that perhaps the wolf signified my sensitivity and need for independence, while remaining loyal to those closest to me. Loyalty to family and friends is paramount, but the need to occasionally leave my pack to explore the wilderness is a major part of who I am. My shadow animal seems to be inherently connected to my spirituality, intuition and integrity, and I can now truly see the presence of my wolf in many different aspects of my daily behavioural patterns. For instance, I need to walk in nature each day at some point. If I don't, I feel stressed, as if I have refused or repressed the part of me that needs to 'roam'. At night, I always feel a strong desire to step outside and gaze up at the stars, and in that moment, I feel complete and totally at peace. My brain is constantly thinking strategically; when I'm outside I'm highly aware of everything that is happening around me, and I have always had a propensity to assess potential dangers.

Interestingly, the moment I brought my shadow animal into my consciousness, I felt more in tune with my senses, as if they'd suddenly been heightened. It stands to reason that we may often repress an aspect of ourselves through the conditioning of what society or environment tell us we should or shouldn't be; the exercise I'm about to show you 'Walking with Your Shadow Animal' will help you reconnect to the more primal, honest and spiritual part of yourself.

EXERCISE: WALKING WITH YOUR SHADOW ANIMAL

- On your next walk, I want you to think that if you were suddenly transformed into an animal, which would you be? Why have you chosen this animal and what aspects of it do you like? How do you feel others would react to this animal? What basic needs does it have? What are your animal's favourite environments and which ones help it to thrive? How do you feel your animal would fare in your current environments, both at work and at home?

- As you walk, I now want you to observe nature through the eyes of your shadow animal, and to try and truly encapsulate their spirit, intuition and power. Would they be exploring, hunting for food, wandering playfully, focusing on their journey ahead, or connecting and looking mindfully at different objects they encounter?

- At the end of your walk, make a note of what came into your mind intuitively as your shadow animal. What message did your shadow animal leave behind, and what aspects of its character do you connect with retrospectively?

- Which of these aspects do you feel you would like to now carry forward and incorporate into your personal and professional life? Envisage how your life could be affected by implementing these new-found qualities. Take a moment to sit with the feelings that accompany this future vision of your more powerful self.

I walked through this exercise with Matt. He laughed when I asked him to consider what his spirit animal might be. 'I'm not sure I should tell you,' he said, 'It's probably not what you'd expect . . .'

I pressed him further. 'OK, here goes,' he said. 'It would be the donkey.'

I smiled, fascinated by his choice. 'Amazing, and not the most conventional spirit animal,' I said. 'But let's find out what's behind it.'

Matt explained he'd been drawn to the donkey since childhood. 'I used to love a donkey ride at the seaside,' he said. 'They always seemed patient, no matter how many kids sat on their backs each day. There was always something "knowing" about them, though. I never thought they were the dumb, passive creatures people made them out to be.'

In his Walking Diary, Matt expanded on his theme:

I like the donkey because it represents strength, solidity and a willingness to carry burdens uncomplainingly. It's a gentle creature, though it doesn't suffer fools. Think of the power of a mule's kick when it's annoyed!

As a shadow animal, what aspects of it do I relate to? It has a broad back, and so do I. I 'carry' a lot of stuff about; I'm a very good listener and people very often unburden their troubles to me. Does that mean I take on too much? Maybe . . . Do I need set boundaries around how much I take on? Yes, probably.

The donkey is stubborn, and I admire that. It will carry out tasks to the end, but if it really doesn't want to do something, it refuses to budge. I think this is a useful trait sometimes. Other times, maybe I've been *too* stubborn and said 'No' when a 'Yes' might have opened a few doors. Again, it's down to boundaries and what feels comfortable.

Matt's insights are interesting because he connects with both the positive and negative aspects of his spirit animal: he acknowledges the strength and resilience of the donkey, while understanding that sometimes he needs to put up boundaries against being overburdened.

Connections and communities

I've mentioned that the early awakening of my spirituality occurred in church. As a child, I recognised the power of a community of people coming together (in my case, a church congregation) for a spiritual purpose and connecting on a level that was something beyond just passing the time of day in the street. Much later, when I was attending AA meetings, I understood what being with other people can achieve when I acknowledged the help and support of my fellow attendees.

As a musician, I've also seen how the power of music transcends space and time and connects with large groups of people on a deep, primal level. As we are growing in the womb, we all hear our mothers' heartbeats rhythmically sounding – I believe this is why music in general, and drumming in particular, connect with us so deeply. There is also the rhythm of walking: when you hear the steady and repetitive crunch of autumn leaves underfoot or the occasional splash from puddles. Or when you stride across the shoreline and your walking corresponds with the ebb and flow of the tide.

The 'higher power'

Think of a community as an ancient tribe that shares everything. We share experience and wisdom and in return we receive love and support. In this highly individualistic world, it can feel daunting to connect with a community, but if we do, we find we open up to people from all walks of life. The importance of this cannot be overstated; you might choose to join a 'silent' walking group which walks meditatively or you may tag along with a group of chatty friends and their dogs who will invariably end their walks at a local pub. Either way, the connections you're making deepen your spiritual sense of self and help you to understand the relevance of what might be termed a 'higher power'. For some, the 'higher power' could be the notion of God as seen by the world's major religions. Others may understand it to be something bigger than us: the stars, the wind, the waves, mountains, trees, wild animals – anything that provides perspective. And it may not be something that feels elemental and 'above' us. It could even be your elderly next-door neighbour, who was a child during World War Two and remembers how it felt to live in a city that was being bombed – an experience that hopefully none of us will ever have to live through, but one which gives us perspective none the less.

Jerry's experience of Walking Therapy has turned up something very interesting and unexpected in his life that has given him a spiritual awakening. It's worth reproducing his account of this at length, as his observations while walking in his London neighbourhood have gifted him a profound sense of peace:

Walking at a deliberate pace helps me notice things for the first time. You see things in your own neighbourhood you swear weren't there yesterday. And I was noticing for the first time that there are churches everywhere. I don't know how I never saw them – I suppose they weren't relevant to my life.

So I started exploring these churches on my walks to work, and sometimes I sat in the pews and just breathed it in. To my total astonishment, an interest in religion sparked from this and now I attend services at my local parish church every Sunday.

It sounds so obvious – and I guess it is obvious to
anyone involved in organised religion – but what I
discovered was that in the heart of our city are
these places that encourage mindful reflection
and contemplation of a higher power; they were
built for it! And it just made me chuckle a bit to
recall how for years, there I was at home building
my own sacred nook to practise mindful medita-
tion in. That was great, but how powerful it has
been to find these safe, warm, communal sacred
spaces. Sanctuaries for everyone, rich or poor.
And exploring these churches on my walks I real-
ised that you don't step back in time in these old,
rooted places, you step out of time, and you
connect to something eternal.
Jerry

Jerry's experience of the 'eternal' and the concept of time is interesting, not least because wherever we walk, we're subconsciously connecting with the footsteps of those who have gone before us. These footsteps could come from someone using the path an hour previously – or it could have been walked upon 10,000 years before we arrived.

Using our imagination to understand this is a very profound way of connecting with the present, and what's happening for us at this moment. Wherever we walk, we walk alongside our ancestors – those people whose day-to-day lives were filled with hope, fear, distraction, suffering, joy, depression, elation and all the rest. These might have been based on very different circumstances, but as humans we have been experiencing life's highs and lows for many millennia. Everything changes over time, and yet nothing does. Knowing this can be a source of great comfort for those of us who feel our difficulties are unique to us, or that we're alone with them.

A path with a story

The past is all around us, and very often literally under our feet. Walking along ancient tracks or following paths of pilgrimage between cathedral cities and tracing old 'coffin routes' across bleak tracts of moorland has become very popular in recent years. Also, I've found myself wandering down some of the timeless streets of old London that feel untouched, and my imagination has been immediately transported back in time, as I wondered how life would have been more than a hundred years ago, filling me with intrigue and excitement. Similarly, a friend recently told me that he enjoys walking along disused railway lines – places where man's ingenuity had to work with nature to get people to their destinations.

EXERCISE: WALKING THROUGH THE PAST

This exercise will take a little planning, but choose a route that you intuitively connect with, or one that fills you with fascination.

- Before you set off on your walk, do some research into the route. Who lived here, and how long ago? What do we know about these people?
- As you walk, try to imagine the scene as it was when past generations lived here. What do you think their hopes and fears were?
- If possible, walk slowly and mindfully, and try to tune into any energy you feel emerging from this place.

- Take note of your senses. What do you see/hear/smell, etc.? Might you be experiencing sensations that those who were here before experienced? If so, how does that make you feel?
- At the end of your walk, allow yourself a quiet moment to give thanks to all those who have gone before – for the wisdom of their experience and for what they have 'shared' with you on this spiritual walk.

In essence, spirituality or connectedness is simply about the deepening of our lives through understanding and experience, leading to the acquisition of wisdom. Whether it takes place in a splendid medieval cathedral, a winding cobbled street in a historic town or city, or on a lonely Roman road is immaterial. What we are seeking is a sense that we are part of everything, and everything is part of us.

To fully connect with the world, we need to slow down, and venture out. We can't connect with anything if we're racing ahead all the time. If we open our eyes, we will suddenly be able to connect with the many different aspects of this world we're surrounded by on a daily basis. But if we continue to move too fast, life will quite literally pass us by, and we will remain disconnected from ourselves and others. We can connect with all that is around us any time we choose; we just need to give ourselves the permission to do so.

CHAPTER 11: MAINTENANCE FOR MIND, BODY AND SPIRIT

Ever tried? Ever failed? No matter. Try again. Fail better.
Samuel Beckett, Irish novelist and playwright (1906–89)

We've now reached a point in this book where I can, meta-phorically, let go of your hand and watch you walk off down the path to a happier and healthier life. If you've been following the advice I've outlined, you're more than likely to be a good way down that path already, and I hope your journey continues to bring you the benefits and rewards you've been looking for.

The question is: can you put in the effort and determination required to keep up your walking programme and maintain the goals you've achieved thus far? Will you continue to walk with your wolf (or whatever your wild creature is), and sustain the vital connection you've made to nature that will continue to protect, nurture and guide you through the rest of your life?

The answer, I hope, is 'Yes'. But before we congratulate ourselves, let's check in with reality for a moment. Because the truth is, maintaining and sustaining early success isn't easy. During our journey, we've explored many of the reasons people are reluctant to take time out for themselves, and while you now understand these with reference to your own life, you are going to have to be vigilant, strong and disciplined if you are to uphold this time and space you've set aside for yourself each week.

Why? Because life will challenge you and force you, at times, to compromise your boundaries. You may find yourself under pressure once again to say 'Yes, I will' when you really meant to say 'No, I can't'. You might find yourself frequently fighting the 'shaming' voice that tells you what you 'should be' and 'ought to be' doing, instead of doing the things which nurture you. There will be times when you think, 'Forget it, I don't want to walk today,' as you, once again, go in search of other distractions. And there will be other times when you do walk, and feel you've learned nothing from the experience.

The importance of diarising

Writing this book has emphasised time and time again for me the importance of personal boundaries. And diarising is essentially the action of setting personal boundaries for yourself. You should never, ever feel guilty about making reasonable time for yourself, and if others try to shame you into thinking or acting otherwise, then you should change the nature of that relationship, or end it completely.

To help you maintain the discipline of protecting time for yourself, always remember to *diarise*. Make it extremely clear to yourself and others by writing down, on paper or in whatever online calendar you use, that on *this* day, at *this* time, you will not be available. That way, you set in stone the commitment you're making to yourself and you gain the respect of others for setting clear boundaries. This is vital in an age where life has speeded up immeasurably, and the demands on our time are ever-increasing. Think of a boundary as a safety perimeter. When we feel safe, we feel calm. The same goes for animals

– it is only when an animal feels properly secure, and safe from any threats or dangers, that it can fully relax.

Personally speaking, if I don't have my boundaries, I feel overwhelmed and internally chaotic. If this happens, I soon start making chaotic decisions which increase my stress levels and result in the loss of my personal clarity. Chaos will always create drama, so boundaries give me order and manageability in my day-to-day life, and I know that if I don't diarise it, it won't happen.

So set things up and stick to them. Put aside an hour for yourself each day in your diary to start with. It might seem hard, but it really isn't. Just try it and see. If you can maintain your boundaries and have a good amount of time in the day to connect with yourself, your life will be vastly different within a short period of time.

Setting boundaries, taking a back seat by letting someone else take control or responsibility and not having all the answers, was key to my recovery. It brought a calm to life that I'd never had; plus, ironically, I felt more a man than I ever did when I was 'running the world'.
Elliot

Honesty and integrity

A big part of our maintenance is about honesty. Being clear about what you need to lead a balanced and happy life starts with being honest and communicating this to yourself and others. For instance, if you're explicit about your boundaries (such as diarising your time), you're demonstrating your honesty and your basic needs. It's all too easy to make excuses to yourself (and others) for not doing something, but excuses are incompatible with honesty. If this book is about anything, it's about the search for the authentic self, and honesty plays a big part in that. If you're honest during your exploration of self, you will find yourself making fewer and fewer excuses. Being honest helps you to remake a connection with your core value system, that part of you which has been lost to stress, compromise and fear. So if you do make excuses for not walking or lowering your boundaries, at least be honest about them.

Honesty and the quest for the authentic self can quite often lead to more questions than answers. Maintaining the lessons learned in this book will inevitably force you to look at the life you're currently living and whether it is compatible with your authentic self.

You know that a lot of life's stresses and strains arise at work – the place you spend so much of your daily life. If you realise your workplace is incompatible with your authentic self, then you need to consider changing it completely, or at least putting boundaries in place to make sure you aren't overburdened. Such boundaries might involve immersing yourself in one thing at a time and stopping multitasking. 'Keep life simple' is a key phrase, and if those around you can't understand that, then it's time to consider a change. All the clients in this book recognised the damage their work-places were doing, and either changed jobs or made sure they laid down firm boundaries. If they can do it, so can you. And if you're reading this thinking, 'Easy for him to say; he's nowhere near as busy as I am', then think again. I work full-time and am a father of two girls who, at the time of writing, are both under five years old. So trust me, I have my hands full. But I have an active life and stand by all that I relay to you, so you're not on your own.

Reaching out

As well as reaching into your own depths in order to heal, it is important that you reach out to others. I've spoken about everyone's need for communities they can rely upon as a source of love, support and nurture. Life is rarely constant, and when change happens it is the support network you have built which will take you through such transitions. I'm a lone wolf, but it has been other people who've put me back on the right track. As much as I love the sanctuary of being on my own, I wouldn't be here but for other people and their empathy. In that respect, we need to reach out to others, do things that connect us to different aspects of the world, different lives, different perspectives. In my mind's eye, I see a lighthouse built on a rock, standing solid against the raging storm and crashing waves. Yet what use is a lighthouse without someone to switch on the light for the benefit of others? If it remains unlit, it is just another hazard for ships. But if the lighthouse keeper does their job and maintains the light, it is for the good of the whole community. We should be that lighthouse keeper, extending our light, reaching out to others immersed in their own sea of troubles.

To this end, ask yourself, 'How can I be of use to others?' What can you do for the benefit of other people that will also help with your confidence, improve your life skills and assist in your quest for the authentic self? Receiving all the benefits I've outlined through Walking Therapy is great, but it's when you start to give back that you truly discover a sense of purpose and positivity. Giving comes with a warm glow that each of us carries – one that will lovingly support you and others through all manner of setbacks and challenges. It will also open you up to those you may not previously have considered as 'my kind of people'. Too often, we push certain people away because we feel we don't have a connection with them. Yet, they might be really crying out for your help and if you choose to answer that cry, you are doing something extremely powerful, both for yourself and the person who needs help. Who knows – the person you might have considered pushing away might hold the key to something that changes your life completely, and for the better. You will never know unless you answer the call.

WALKING AND BASIC LISTENING SKILLS

As you've been walking, you've learned to listen to yourself. Now I'm going to give you a quick lesson in how to listen to others, either while you're out walking with them or in a situation where someone is asking for your help or advice. (**Note:** this is where I give away all the invaluable secrets of my success!)

- Empathy and sympathy. Learn to understand the difference between the two. Being sympathetic means objectively feeling sorrow or pity for someone's troubles. Being empathetic is about subjectively stepping into that person's shoes and understanding their troubles from the inside out. Which do you think is the most useful?
- Be non-judgemental. This does require objectivity. Try not to bring your own likes, dislikes, prejudices, politics, etc. to the situation. Hear what's going on for that person as an individual. Don't introduce your own agenda to what you think the other person needs to do based on your own life experience.
- Be present. Don't just wait your turn to speak – really *listen* to what's being said.

- Be patient. Don't rush the person who is speaking. By hurrying them along, you will more than likely close them down. Let their words breathe.
- Rescuing and fixing. Don't! It is counterproductive to push someone towards an immediate solution, as this may take time. Allow that time to unfold.
- Reflecting and summarising. Again, don't fix. Instead, reflect on what has been said and summarise this, so you're both on the same page.

Therapists in general tend not to share their own life stories or troubles with clients but, as I said much earlier, I don't stand by this archaic rule, and where appropriate I share my experiences with the people I work with, just as I've shared them with you in this book. I try not to overshare, but I do try to identify lightly with my clients' issues, as in the last of the basic listening skills above. I try to show them where I've strayed from the path and what has brought me back to it; we're all human, even therapists,

Self-care – fuel for body and mind

Like any machine, the body needs the right type and amount of fuel to maintain its efficiency, and it must be of a high standard too. As my personal trainer says to me time and again, 'Jonathan, you need to feed the machine'.

I love good food and I love cooking, but I noticed that during my walks, my sugar levels were nosediving, which affected me physically (feeling faint and disassociated) and psychologically. This made me wonder about the extent to which what we eat affects our mental health. I approached nutritional therapist and clinical hypnotherapist Nicola Shubrook for help with transforming my diet and here is the essence of what she explained to me (for more information from Nicola, visit www.urbanwellness.co.uk).

According to Nicola, fuelling the body with high-sugar foods spikes our blood glucose too quickly and every time it wears off, it crashes, bringing our energy and our moods crashing down with it. I remember feeling this way the morning after drinking alcohol, which is packed with sugar. Even a few glasses of wine after work would cause my sugar levels to crash at around three in the morning, inevitably waking me up and badly affecting my sleep cycle (circadian rhythm).

Nicola describes the 'rollercoaster' of sugar, which, after an initial 'high', can make you angry, depressed, more likely to overreact or feel more stressed than you were before as it triggers your fight, flight or freeze response (see p. 17). In other words, more sugar creates more stress, which hinders your ability to get an adequate night's sleep and function properly the next day. Excess sugar in your diet vastly decreases levels of serotonin, 'the happy hormone', which you need to help regulate mood and social behaviour.

Blood-sugar balancing also plays an important role in exercise. Which brings us to walking.

To stay present during your walks (and any time), eating the rights foods is essential. This will support those blood sugars and help to stabilise your mood. It's not about 'cutting the carbs', as they are the body's first source of energy; it's about the *right carbs* and eating them together with two other essential food macronutrients: protein and fat.

Here are some suggestions to help replenish mind and body before, during and after walking:

Food

Good protein supplies can be found in animal sources, such as meat, fish, eggs and full-fat dairy products, as well as plant sources, which include nuts, seeds, peas, lentils, beans and tofu. The 'good fats' include olive oil, avocados, nuts and seeds, coconut oil and butter, as well as oily fish such as salmon, mackerel, anchovies and sardines. These fish, as well as chia seeds, flaxseeds and walnuts, contain omega-3, a nutrient that plays an important role in supporting good mental health, and may also be of benefit in the prevention of conditions such as depression, anxiety, PTSD and bipolar. As for the carbs, think high-fibre – so vegetables, fruit (not fruit juice), oats, quinoa, brown or wild rice, lentils, beans, potatoes (white or sweet and ideally with their skin on) and root vegetables such as parsnips and squash.

Water

Another important factor in managing mood, energy and stress levels is water. Technically, we can last weeks without food, but only a few days without water, and yet few of us drink enough. Dehydration is also thought to vastly increase cortisol levels and worsen how you feel both mentally and physically, just like food. Add excess caffeine, alcohol and even drug use into the mix and these effects will be exacerbated.

The ideal amount of water needed per day is the subject of ongoing debate, but for most people, around 1–1.5 litres a day is a good start. That's plain water that hasn't been sweetened with squash and doesn't include any tea or coffee intake. Staying hydrated when walking, or embarking on any exercise, is vital in not only supporting energy levels, but also preventing injury and cramp. Your body will naturally lose water when walking, so it is important to follow these guidelines:

- Drink about half a litre before you walk in order that your body takes on what it needs and any excess can be flushed out when you go to the toilet before you set off.
- Limit your caffeine intake, as it may make you thirstier and increase the need for the toilet when out walking.
- Keep sipping water throughout your walk to keep properly hydrated.
- Post-walk, drink another half a litre to replenish stores. You may also want to add a little salt to your snack or meal to replace any salts lost through sweating.

Sleep hygiene

If you're tired, and don't have adequate rest, your body and mind simply cannot function properly, which tends to leave you feeling more vulnerable, so your nervous system generates a stress response (anxiety or hyperarousal) to inform and alert you to the fact that your body requires something. Here are a few key tips to ensure better sleep hygiene:

1. Give your body the right levels and types of protein throughout the day. For example, milk, and milk products contain tryptophan, which is a sleep-inducing amino acid.
2. Decrease your sugar intake as this helps to lower cortisol levels, thereby improving the quality of your sleep.

3. Take adequate breaks throughout the day to prevent your body from producing too much adrenalin and cortisol – this will greatly help to decrease mental and physical stress at night.
4. Avoid caffeine and alcohol completely in the evening.
5. Switch off technology. Looking at bright screens before bed can stop your brain producing melatonin, the hormone that tells your body when it's time to sleep.

The above advice is terrific for maintaining and enhancing what we're already receiving from Walking Therapy. After integrating all of this into my own regime, the results have been staggering. Every morning, I am filled with energy because I'm sleeping so much better. My sugar levels are no longer nosediving during my daily walks, and at the end of them, I feel as energised as when I first set off. My concentration has greatly improved too, and this has helped me to feel more present throughout the course of each day. I'm not sure why, but my eyesight has also improved, and all in all, my body feels like a much more effective machine. I would advise you to give this a go and to reap the benefits, as I have.

Walking, failing and walking again

Finally – allow yourself to fail. There will be times when you don't want to walk. Times when you will just sit there, feeling unmotivated and dispirited. You might crack and have that bottle of wine or packet of cigarettes that does you no good. You might say 'Yes' to doing something when you really mean 'No'. You will relax your boundaries and regret doing so. Don't worry – it happens to us all. No one is superhuman, and those who make such a claim may need to take a good look at themselves.

We all mess up. I've fallen off the wagon, strayed from the path, lost sight of why I'm doing all this. But I haven't beaten myself up about it. I have not shamed myself. Instead, I've been honest, dusted myself off and learned from my mistakes. Perseverance and resilience are key to living and adapting. If the wolf fails to secure its prey during a hunting session, it doesn't dwell on its failure. It simply doesn't have the capacity for that. Instead, it goes hungry for a night and then, the following day, it renews its quest for food with vigour.

FINAL THOUGHTS

Now we're at the end of the book, and our walk together is coming to an end. I can't promise that the path on which I hope you continue will be straight, unbroken and smooth. Paths, like life, tend not to be that way. They are rutted and potholed, often dog-legged and sometimes lead nowhere. The destination can be unpredictable, and you might not end up where you'd hoped. Still, the quality of the journey and the lessons learned on the way count for everything.

Let's be honest – the self-help/motivational book industry is a big one, precisely because people give up on one thing and go in search of another means of fixing themselves. There are many people who read dozens, even hundreds of such books and still return to the same question: 'Why am I feeling this way?'

I'm not here to tell you that this is the only book you'll ever need. But if you have arrived at the question above, you really need to take a hard look at your determination and commitment to work on yourself for the changes you'd like to see in your life. So let me spell it out in a way you're unlikely to read in 99.9 per cent of self-help titles: *If you've committed to this book, great. If you haven't, take accountability for your actions, go back to the very beginning and this time . . . COMMIT TO IT.*

It's time to stop blaming others, and start taking responsibility for your actions. I don't apologise for pulling punches. You've invested in this book financially and taken the time to read thus far. This is about *making a commitment to you.* Be selfish. Be self-caring. It's an unfashionable attitude, perhaps, but you, and you alone, are fully responsible for what happens next. If you can't or won't take that responsibility, and you find that others march across your boundaries while you remain at square one, then what do you expect? And if you're now saying to yourself, 'It's not the right time in my life to make these changes', think again. It *is* the right time – that's just fear talking. Be brave enough to make clear and positive life choices for *you*; continue to push yourself out of your comfort zone, and you can make anything happen if you want it enough.

Yes, you need guts to open up to your own vulnerability and talk about your feelings. And courage to act on those feelings and make changes – sometimes quite profound ones – to your life. To unstick yourself from your circumstances, you need to be bold and self-assured; but with confidence, you can tune out those who would keep you in your place and not worry whether you have 'permission' from these same people (or yourself) to make the changes you need to grow. Actually – if you *do* need permission I'm giving it to you right now. And remember: the worst trauma occurs not when we're abandoned by others, but when we abandon ourselves.

With such power comes responsibility. Take responsibility for your thoughts and actions, and act on them as you see fit. If there are hiccups, difficulties, forks in the road, don't blame others. This is your path now – be accountable to yourself for the journey you're on. And don't overthink it. As someone once said to me, 'Do now, understand later.'

So just to recap, remember the three core Walking Therapy components:

- **Psychological:** walking helps you to relax your mind and process your feelings more effectively.
- **Physiological:** walking keeps your body in physically good shape, decreasing blood pressure and helping you lose weight.
- **Spiritual:** walking gives you a sense of inner peace and a feeling of connectedness, being nurtured and protected by nature.

Walking regularly will help you to build the courage, confidence and sense of responsibility you need to change your life. If you feel down, stressed, unhealthy, depressed, grief-stricken or addicted to something, my advice is simple, and the same as it was at the start of this book: get outside, go for a walk and notice the difference it makes. If even this simple act makes you fearful, don't worry. We all feel like that. If you're scared, share your fears with a friend, a partner or someone who will support you unconditionally and non-judgementally, as nature did for me in a non-verbal spiritual sense. Fear can inhibit you, but it can also sharpen your senses. If the wolf had no fear, it wouldn't last long in the wild. A little fear is no bad thing, but don't let it become a tidal wave that drowns you. In many respects, you need to learn how to surf fear, and use it to propel you forward in your life.

All those who contributed to this book have felt fear at some point in their lives, and still do now and again. Yet to understand and manage fear, you have to experience it first-hand, not shy away from it. Our contributors pushed on because they knew that somewhere through their tunnel of fear, stress or depression was the pinprick of light they were seeking. For them, the life changes they made were worth the journey through the darkness and gloom:

- Beverley is aware when she is feeling burnt out and has put clear boundaries around herself.
- Elliot no longer pushes himself to the limit and lives a much happier, healthier life as a result.
- Francis accepts the loss of his best friend and carries her wisdom in his heart.
- Jerry walks every day and continues to explore the awakened spiritual side of his personality.
- Katrina is in a great job where she is valued.
- Matt is learning to live by himself, for himself.
- Ryan has come to terms with his sexuality and married his partner.
- Tianna writes regularly, impressing friends with her poetry.
- Victoria's assertiveness has gone from strength to strength and she now understands how to achieve balance in her life.
- Winston is feeling more confident about what he needs to implement in his life, which has given him hope for the future.

For me, one of the biggest pointers to the seismic changes our contributors have made in their lives is that they're not scared to speak out about what they went through, how it affected them and what they needed to do to find their paths. By talking about their difficulties, they have eradicated shame from their narrative. That also takes courage, but as they say, a trouble shared is a trouble halved. And when you feel your troubles lessening, take time to appreciate how far you've come, and what you've achieved. Walk, and at some point, take a break and write down all the things you feel grateful for. This doesn't have to be a long list, but quite often it ends up that way.

As a final exercise, let's have a look at what our core values and beliefs look like now we've reached the end of this book. The development of such beliefs throughout our lives is usually based upon how we're parented, what we witness in society during our upbringing and how we're introduced to the world during our formative years. The world is either presented to us as a safe or an unsafe place. However, we can challenge and change our core belief and value systems at any time. With this in mind, let's now create our ten 'Life Principles'.

EXERCISE: IDENTIFYING OUR LIFE PRINCIPLES

The idea here is to clarify what you would like your values and beliefs to look like in the future. Here are some questions you could ask yourself:

- What makes me feel passionate and excited?
- What drives and motivates me?
- What are my likes and dislikes?
- What are some of my life philosophies?
- What particularly irritates me and why?
- What ethos do I live by now?
- What would I change in the world and why?
- What currently makes my life happy? And what makes me unhappy?
- Is there anything a friend or family member has done recently to upset or irritate me, and why is that?
- What currently inspires me and why?

In hindsight, where do you see your old beliefs clashing with your new ones? And moving forward, what changes do you need to make to achieve more positive results in

---

the future? At the end of your walk, once you've given the above questions some due consideration and thought, I would like you to write down and consolidate what you would like your ten Life Principles to be going forward. Once these are developed, and you're happy with your new set of principles, every time you go for a walk, ask yourself how you are carefully integrating and implementing them into your life.

My advice will always be to create a quality of life for yourself that has a simple design, and values you can truly stand by. Declutter, travel light and enjoy the freedom that leaving excess baggage behind brings to your life.

Finally, let's return to the animal that has guided us through this book, sometimes in daylight, sometimes in shadow. Every day that I walk with my wolf I feel its presence guiding me, influencing the choices I make and the actions I take. The wolf is powerful and intuitive, yet at the same time vulnerable and subject to the stresses and strains of life. It looks strong but doesn't always feel it. Even so, the wolf knows where its strength comes from and how to reconnect with that. Below are a few words I wrote in response to the inspiration and strength that the wolf gives me every day:

Lying head down under a pale moon, the wolf seemed fearful and overwhelmed by the almost insurmountable tasks that surviving in the wild brings. But as he took a moment to observe the vast wilderness lying peacefully beneath a blanket of stars, majestic and benevolent in its beauty, he sighed, 'I understand now. My family is not just among my pack. My family is in the wind, among the trees, upon the earth and in the sky. How long have they been residing within the light that shines on my face at night, and within the warmth of the sun that awakens my spirit each moment of every day? From this point onwards, when I choose to truly see and connect with my family, I will know that there is no need for me to feel alone or afraid.'

And as the wolf wandered slowly forward into the unknown, he whispered, 'I will overcome. I will have the intuition, integrity and insight to negotiate a secure path for my future. A path that will help me to dismantle all fears and obstacles stemming from my past, encouraging me to confront each of them in turn, as I refuse to sidestep my fear of the unknown.'

And with a slight turn of his head, he was gone.

Thank you for coming on this journey with me, and all the very best of luck for your own.

All good wishes,
Jonathan Hoban

ACKNOWLEDGEMENTS

I would firstly like to thank my wife Shereen for her love, devotion and unwavering support through thick and thin, and my beautiful daughters Aria and Amelie for the joy they bring to my life. I am infinitely grateful too for the love and support of other members of my immediate family.

A special thanks to my literary agent Jaime Marshall for going above and beyond the call of duty in overseeing all aspects of making this book possible, from beginning to end, and to Tom Henry for his creative literary skills, input and guidance on this project. I feel blessed to have been surrounded and to have benefited from their knowledge, expertise and years of literary experience.

This book wouldn't have been possible without the expertise, insight and hard work of Liz Gough, Becca Mundy, Holly Whitaker and the whole amazing Yellow Kite team (including my talented freelance copyeditor Anne Newman, part of the extended team). I thank every one of them for believing in this book and for making it happen. Also, a massive thanks to my independent publicist Mary Jones for working with me and the Yellow Kite team to help make this book become known to the world at large.

Without my manager Ronan O'Rahilly and the belief he instilled in me, I wouldn't have become the person I am today and I wouldn't have followed my dreams. My mother and father have my eternal love and respect for bringing me safely into this world and providing me with so many happy childhood memories and experiences. If I can be even a quarter of the type of parent they were to us all, I will count myself extremely fortunate. They were very special people and I continue to be inspired by the memory of them every day.

Thank you to Anne Carroll MBE, who was my drama teacher before I became a musician. After my mother died, she sat me down backstage, looked at me, and with such love and attentiveness said 'Jonny, I can't imagine what you're feeling, only that it can't be easy. If you need anything, just let me know.' And then with a cheeky wry smile that only she knew how to pull off, said 'Now, in the meantime, why don't you go out there and give the best performance of your life so that your emotion has somewhere to go. Really give it some!' Bless her. To this very day, I have never forgotten her kindness or how she taught me about the power of a kind word or two. Thanks, Anne.

To all the counsellors, organisers and the peer group at SHARP Drug and Alcohol Rehabilitation Centre, I wish there were more 12-Step programmes like this one. What I learnt within three months at this place still reverberates through my mind and definitely helped me to define my style as a therapist. But a very special thank you has to go to one of my counsellors, Cathy Lewis, who provided me with true unconditional support and guidance through one of my most difficult, turbulent and lengthy life transitions. The level of empathy she gave me over the years made me realise that this was indeed the antidote to shame. The insight derived from this experience has become central to my work ever since.

Finally, thank you to all the wonderful participants in the book who decided to make the necessary changes to lead a better life. It's because of you, and your courage to undergo this process, that I remain constantly inspired to do this wonderful job of mine. How lucky am I!

REFERENCES

1. www.pnas.org/content/early/2015/06/23/1510459112
2. www.mentalhealth.org.uk/news/stressed-nation-74-uk-overwhelmed-or-unable-cope-some-point-past-year
3. www.theguardian.com/society/2018/may/14/three-in-four-britons-felt-overwhelmed-by-stress-survey-reveals
4. Health and Safety Executive Labour Force Survey 2016/17
5. Lydon, J. (1986) *Rise*, Virgin
6. www.ons.gov.uk/peoplepopulationandcommunity/healthandsocialcare/drugusealcoholandsmoking/datasets/adultdrinkinghabits

yellow
kite

books to help you live a good life

Join the conversation and tell
us how you live a #goodlife

🐦 @yellowkitebooks
f YellowKiteBooks
📌 Yellow Kite Books
📷 YellowKiteBooks